— 1983 —
8²⁵

FAMILIES, ALCOHOLISM AND RECOVERY

ABOUT THE BOOK:

Families with an alcoholic member develop ways of adapting to each other and their environment that are as unhealthy for the rest of the family as for the alcoholic. Truly effective therapy for the alcoholic *and* for the family member must take into account these systems of interactions.

Through her judicious interspersing of family systems counseling theory with illustrative case studies, Ms. Dulfano has created a book that will serve as an informative guide for those who counsel and treat the alcoholic and the family members.

ABOUT THE AUTHOR:

Celia Dulfano, M.S.W., is Clinical Associate Professor of the Department of Psychiatry at the State University of New York and is associated with the Downstate Medical Center in Brooklyn, New York. She teaches Family Therapy at the Summer School of Alcohol Studies at Rutgers University and continues to counsel in private practice.

FAMILIES, ALCOHOLISM, AND RECOVERY

Ten Stories

Celia Dulfano, M. S. W.

First printing, April 1982.

ISBN: 0-89486-148-4

Printed in the United States of America.

To
Yakito, Shevy, Guila, David, and Asaph

CONTENTS

PREFACE

In the relatively brief history of the treatment of alcoholism as a facet of health care, the concept of providing services for the families of alcoholics has an even briefer history. In recent years, we in the field of alcoholism treatment have acknowledged the fact that the family does need assistance. In this book, Celia Dulfano demonstrates how family interactions and family systems affect the recovery from alcoholism for the entire family. She illustrates the concept of contextual relationships and shows their importance in facilitating a new understanding for the whole family.

Celia Dulfano exhibits her sensitivity to alcoholism as a condition which exists in relationship to other family members and shows how significantly they are involved in the condition. Not only does the identified alcoholic need help in responding to the condition, but each family member in turn needs help.

By using simple, realistic examples, Ms. Dulfano is able to create pathways through the contextual maze. Her ability to communicate a systems model with the goal of a "changed family" is the strength of this book.

Daniel J. Anderson, Ph.D.
President, Director
Hazelden Foundation
April, 1982

ACKNOWLEDGMENTS

This book is an outgrowth of my experiences working in the field of alcoholism for the past 20 years. During this time I had contact with many families, professionals and students. I want to thank all of them for adding to my growth as a person and as a therapist.

My special thanks to Gladys M. Price who introduced me to the field of alcoholism, while I was a student at the Washingtonian Hospital, in Boston, Massachusetts, and who has continued to be my mentor, colleague, and friend.

I was extremely fortunate to have had the skillful help of Frances Hitchcock who played a very important role in editing this book.

Richard Edelman, trustee of the Matz Foundation, Edelman Division, New York, has shown continued interest in the development of programs in Family Therapy. His support was crucial for the completion of this book.

My thanks to Margaret M. Heyman and Viola R. Isaacs, colleagues and friends, for critical comments and revisions of the manuscript.

And to my husband for his caring and assistance throughout my career.

Introduction

Alcoholism and Family

When Peter Richardson* was ten, his school referred him to the pediatric department of a community hospital. Peter's teachers complained that he was impossible to reach. He was always either withdrawn and daydreaming, or disrupting the class with nervous activity that he seemed totally unable to control. He also presented severe reading problems. With these symptoms, the obvious course was to have Peter evaluated by a child psychiatrist. The diagnosis was early schizophrenia.

Peter began individual treatment and remedial reading classes. But both therapists noticed a curious inconsistency. Sometimes Peter came on time for his appointments, related well, and worked hard on his reading assignments. Sometimes he showed up half an hour late with a vague excuse and repeated the daydreaming and/or hyperactivity reported by the school.

A hospital social worker made an appointment to see Peter's mother, Collette. As they shook hands, she smelled liquor on

---

* Names and family circumstances have been changed in every case.

1

Collette's breath, at 11 a.m. The social worker asked Collette if she'd been drinking. Surprised, Collette confided that she had to have a drink before coming to keep the appointment.

As we learned more about the Richardson family, we discovered that both Collette and Sean, Peter's stepfather, were alcoholics. Sean was a steady drinker, but Collette was only intermittently drunk. While sober, she functioned capably as a working mother, supervising Peter's activities, sending him to appointments on time, and, in general, giving him some sense of stability. But when Collette, too, was drinking, Peter went home to a deserted apartment, or to parents who were drunk or passed out. He stayed in the apartment, watching TV, caring for his dog who was his closest companion, making himself a sandwich for dinner, and, whenever necessary, phoning the local liquor store for a delivery. His "early schizophrenic" behavior was the behavior of a child deprived of his parents by the disease of alcoholism.

This is a book about real people, with their desires and sufferings. They are all different, and the selection of cases is not arbitrary. They are case histories from my own practice which illustrate different alcoholism problems and therapeutic solutions. The affected people came into contact with various professional disciplines through a variety of agencies; agencies that did not always identify alcoholism as the primary problem.

These families have all been profoundly affected by alcoholism. But they are also the Harrisons, the O'Briens, the Stewarts. . . I have always felt very uncomfortable about labeling patients. The helping professions, it seems to me, are overused to stereotyping. We even tend to take historical data from the standpoint of an already imposed diagnosis. The diagnosis is alcoholism; therefore, the person behind the diagnosis recedes. This happens to an even greater extent to the families of alcoholics. The alcoholic's wife is not seen as a person. She is not even a patient. She is only the patient's wife.

In emphasizing the problem, the human individualism of the people described is lost. Yet, too much specificity is not useful; an exact report of the treatment of Family Y by Therapist X would be useful only to clones of the Y's and Therapist X, and then only for a short period of time. In writing these case reports, I have tried to steer a course between the two extremes, presenting material in a way that is specific enough to be human, yet generalized enough to be useful. If the reader ends with an understanding of how to look at alcoholism in the family and learns to approach the family as a unit for therapy, the book will have accomplished most of its goals.

Theory vs. Practice: Transitions

The field of alcoholism therapy seems to be in a very interesting, transitional stage. We still tend to zero in on the individual alcoholic, as we have always done. At the same time, it is common knowledge (as it always has been) that alcoholism is a social syndrome. Alcohol is a drug. Abuse of alcohol is an illness. But it is an illness that is deeply interconnected with the current context of the individual's life. Most therapies recognize this, however implicitly. Many therapies involve removing the patient from this context, either in theory or in fact, while therapy is in process.

The development of what have been called ecological therapies, over the past twenty years, has given alcoholism therapy tools for approaching and dealing with the patient's environment. In theory we can now work with both individual and "significant others" in a multi-effort attack on both the intrapsychic and the interpersonal components of the alcoholism syndrome. Unfortunately, this theoretical knowledge has not yet been incorporated into our actual therapeutic structures. When we look into the lives of alcoholics who are in treatment, we find them going from agency to agency, from therapeutic method to therapeutic method, receiving intense input into personal change and growth, but with little help for the actual problems of coping with an unchanged interpersonal context, let alone help in ameliorating that context.

Working with alcoholism in the family is a particularly effective therapeutic method in many cases. This significant interpersonal context can be changed in ways that support the maintenance of sobriety and the reintegration of the sober alcoholic as a coping and competent family member. Furthermore, valuable preventive therapy can be done with people who have experienced the stresses of living with an alcoholic. That this can be done is common knowledge in the field. To find it actually being done is still all too rare.

The Alcoholism Therapist: Changes in Perspectives

As a therapist working with alcoholism in specialized agencies, mental health agencies, and the family therapy division of a psychiatric unit, I have experienced this transitional period in my own professional development. Like most professionals now specializing in alcoholism, I learned the dynamics of the syndrome by working with individual alcoholics. I became acquainted with the vast literature and research on the medical and psychological correlates of alcoholism. Like alcoholics themselves, I have had to learn that alcoholism is an illness, not a sin. Coming from a culture where wine is customarily served with meals, I had to begin by accepting, as part of my own personal beliefs, the concept of alcoholism as a disease.

As I worked with individual alcoholics, I became aware of the consequences of this problem for the alcoholic's family and social network. Over a period of time, I began to recognize that the focus on the individual alcoholic, while not incorrect, was incomplete. The theory underlying alcoholism therapy was that a vulnerable individual, with personal deficits probably combined with physiological predisposition, was escaping personal and social pressures by abusing alcohol. Great efforts, therefore, were put into helping the individual deal with those personal deficits. Sometimes he or she was hospitalized or insitutionalized for medical treatment combined with psychotherapy or behavioral therapy. Sometimes the therapy of choice was group treatment or referral to a self-help organization like Alcoholics Anonymous. In either case I, as the social worker and specialist in alcoholism therapy, coordinated my efforts with the techniques of the psychotherapist, physician, psychologist, behavior therapist, and/or self-help organization in the drive to help the patient attain sobriety. The patient was then, in effect, returned to the environment in which his alcoholism had developed *and expected to maintain sobriety in the face of the unchanged pressures which had combined to exacerbate his problems in the first place.*

As soon as the problem is conceptualized in these terms, of course, an enhanced therapeutic strategy springs to mind. Would it be possible to attack the problems, not only from the standpoint of the individual alcoholic, but also from the standpoint of the interpersonal systems which correlate with the individual's problems? Might it be possible to change salient aspects of the social system?

Like her patients, and like every other human being, a therapist is influenced by her own social network: "Significant others" in my network included family therapists, who helped me to look at individual alcoholics in a new way. I began to apply their ideas to the study and treatment of alcoholism.

Family therapy is one of the theories whose effect can be compared to the discovery of the lever. On the one hand, it seems so simple as to be obvious: everybody knows that people affect each other. On the other hand, the consequences of using this knowledge are so far reaching as to be almost incalculable. When the individual is seen actually interacting within significant social contexts, whole new aspects are opened, not only to conceptualization, but also to therapeutic change.

Salvador Minuchin describes the results of this change of perspective in his anecdote of John. The therapist who sees John, age 14, in the context of individual sessions hears the boy describing a relationship with his mother "which is ambivalent, but with a strong element of attraction." The boy hates his father.

The therapist unravels the history of this process and its repetitive nature throughout the development of the child. He is aware of the boy's anxiety and of his defensive patterns. He interprets the material as an Oedipal conflict with paratactic distortion of the present situation. . .

The context in which the data are gathered shapes not only the data, but also the way the therapist organizes the data.

The therapist who gathers his data in individual sessions will build up an explanation of John's behavior which includes his internalization of his parent figures, the historical development of his conflict with them and the apparently compulsive intrusion of this conflict into extra familial and seemingly unrelated situations in John's life.

But if the therapist sees his 14-year-old "Oedipus" *with* "Jocasta" and "Laius," a different picture emerges.

In [family] interviews, the therapist sees that the relationship of John and Jocasta is characterized by intermingled closeness and hostility. During the sessions most of the communications John sends are directed towards his mother, and even when he does talk to Laius, his father, he seems to do so through his mother, who translates and explains her son to her husband.

The relationship between the spouses is characterized by a lack of intimacy and by very poor communication. There is an absence of marital conflict; disagreements usually are side-tracked into the father's attacking his son for his misbehavior outside the family.

Now the therapist has more than additional data. He also has a new way of organizing data, one which suggests targets for change in the interpersonal process that is feeding into John's "Oedipal conflict."

A similar change in perspective occurs when a therapist looks at an alcoholic in his family context. The rather vague recognition that context affects behavior is immediately replaced by the observation that the alcoholic is part of a significant social system *to which he responds even as it responds to him.* We now accept that alcoholic behavior is a product of factors. The medical aspects of alcoholism, the psychological components of addiction, and the personal deficits are all still part of the picture. But the picture is wider now. It is more complex, but it is also more accurate. The interpersonal transactions of alcoholic and spouse, parent, child, and sibling are now part of the "diagnosis." They are also part of the possibilities for therapy.

"We used to think," wrote Sir Arthur Stanley, "that if we knew one, we knew two, because one and one are two. We are finding that we must learn a great deal more about the 'and.'" The field of alcoholism has recognized that alcoholism is the product of three factors: the biological, the psychological, and the social. What we are doing now is beginning to learn about the "and." Working with families affected by alcoholism is one promising way of learning about that "and." The cases in this book are presented as data for those who want to explore these new directions.

Where Do We Stand Now?

The first steps are largely accomplished. Alcoholism is now generally recognized as an illness; this has been the accomplishment of the past decades. Educational efforts are bringing this knowledge to the public-at-large, though a great deal of work remains to be done in this area. Furthermore, our methods of treating the individual alcoholic have been improved and made more specific by medical and mental health research. Unfortunately, we still tend to focus too narrowly on the individual alcoholic when it comes to therapy. As a result, the effectiveness of our interventions is undercut by the patient's natural environment.

This over-focus on the individual alcoholic has two other consequences as well. First, we are neglecting a large population of people in need of primary mental health care. Second and even worse, we are neglecting opportunities for badly needed preventive therapy.

The spouses, children, parents, and colleagues of the alcoholic are sometimes called the "other victims" of alcoholism. It would be more correct to call them participants in the alcoholic syndrome, but whatever the label, they need our help. They include battered wives and children who live with an alcoholic whose frustration tolerance is low and whose behavior is impulsive and inconsistent. They include children who grow up in families whose functioning is warped by the incapacity of one parent. They include the people undergoing the year-in and year-out stresses of compensating for an alcoholic: The husband trying to support the family and handle housework, child-rearing, and community contacts so well that no one begins to wonder about his wife's "migraine;" The co-workers who cover for good ol' Joe; the babysitter who'll be driven home by a man who's had a few too many, and the driver who may meet them on the road.

Alcoholism is a chronic disease which typically takes ten to fifteen years to develop. By the time an alcoholic comes to therapy, therefore, his family, friends, and associates have been dealing with the impact of progressive alcoholism for years. The children may never have known adequate parenting. The spouse is by definition either over-burdened or, perhaps, defeated. Yet even when their problems are recognized, the nonalcoholic members of these families are too often seen only as adjuncts to the major problem. Their own needs go underattended in the drive to treat the individual alcoholic.

It is little wonder that alcoholism seems to "run in families." Many experts have suggested some hereditary components to alcoholism, and some research indications support this premise. But it is unnecessary to postulate a biological factor to explain why children of alcoholics have difficulties and often become alcoholics themselves. Growing up with an alcoholic parent is quite sufficient to explain its consequences. The chaos in the family, its instability, the lack of an adequate role model, etc., are not the stuff of a healthy childhood.

There are an estimated ten million active alcoholics in the United States alone. We cannot even begin to estimate the number of people affected by these alcoholics. But we will meet some of them in the case examples in this book. How many women, like Irene, growing up with an alcoholic parent, learn to see themselves not as people in their own right, but as adjuncts to some man's problems? How many children, like Joanne, remain over-involved in an alcoholic parent's life long after they should be making lives for themselves? How many boys, like Marty Stewart, deprived of an effective male role model, find it difficult to cope with the world of peers? How many girls, like Carmela Giacomelli, run right home after school to babysit, fix snacks, and start dinner while Mama "naps" on the couch? And aside from the current pain of these situations, how many of these people are "disasters waiting for a place to happen"?

Compensation is possible. We can help these "other victims" develop their own lives as coping individuals. And we can help the individual alcoholic. But then what happens to the family? By working with the individual alcoholic and the alcoholic family, we can do both primary and preventive therapy. In many cases, we can break the patterns that otherwise would entrap this generation and be passed along to the next.

Chapter One

Basic Considerations for Treatment

The causes of alcoholism are multifaceted and deeply rooted. They are also not yet well understood. Nevertheless, alcoholism, the disease, can be combatted therapeutically without a complete understanding of the etiology. It is possible to design effective therapeutic approaches to alcoholism by defining it simply and pragmatically as both an illness that strikes an individual and as a social syndrome which develops over time. In time, parents, spouse, children, extended family members in the alcoholic family, and colleagues and friends in the extrafamilial world, all become part of this social syndrome. They, in turn, affect the alcoholic and his symptoms in a continuing process of interrelating feedback.

Therefore, except in the cases where an alcoholic has become totally estranged from social networks, a therapist intervening with alcoholism in a person is intervening with a whole system of groups. The therapist may never see anyone besides the individual alcoholic, and he may not even be aware of the people he is impacting. But the impact is there. Ideally, the therapist should be aware of this network and interrelate with it. This will make the therapeutic process shorter and more effective while also improving the chances for preventive therapy.

Though it is a chronic disease, alcoholism has acute phases, and it is often an acute crises that brings the alcoholic to the attention of a therapist. The alcoholic has admitted himself to a detoxification unit, or is committed for treatment by a family which has finally reached its limit. Less dramatically, therapy may commence because the alcoholic is threatened with divorce, loss of a job, or perhaps his own sense that his drinking has gone past his control. Sometimes the crisis may be caused by a therapist who recognizes the symptoms of hidden or unacknowledged alcoholism and confronts a patient with them. Therefore, the chronic nature of the disease may not be obvious.

In most cases, the alcoholic has been in difficulty for years. His functioning may have deteriorated steadily, or there may have been long periods of stability only occasionally threatened by uncontrolled drinking. In either case, a whole lifestyle has evolved around this dysfunction, and there is probably a group of people—the patient and his network—whose interactions have been shaped by the problems of alcoholism.

Abundant research has established that biological, psychological, and social components are all present in the etiology of alcoholism. In any given case, these three factors intermesh in the development of the chronic syndrome.

Addictive Components

Alcohol is a depressive psychoactive drug. We tend not to recognize this fact, because alcohol is used socially and is easily available in most places. Nevertheless, it is a drug, and physiological addiction can occur. Frequent ingestion of alcohol builds up tolerance to the drug and gradually larger doses are needed to obtain the same results. The ingestion of continually larger doses bathes the tissues of the central nervous system in high concentrations of the drug, which results eventually in physical dependence. In other words, though alcoholism is a socio-psycho-physiological syndrome, there are components that are purely physiological. Emotional symptoms lead to the excessive drinking, but the increasing physiological dependence, in turn, causes emotional reactions, increasing the rate of drug-seeking behavior on both levels. Without the individual's awareness, he or she becomes dependent on the drug. As tolerance builds, use of alcohol increases, and the craving and need to continue drinking become an unrelenting drive.

Treatment of the physiological components of alcoholism depends very much on the stage of the illness. During its early stages, alcoholism is a symptom. The individual who is developing dependency on alcohol is drinking to relieve some underlying discomfort or to satisfy some underlying needs. The reasons for the drinking, whatever they may be, are the disease; abuse of alcohol is a symptom of that disease. As drinking progresses over the years, however, alcoholism itself becomes the disease. Whatever may have driven the individual to drink in the first place, the cyclic phenomena (tolerance— physiological dependency—loss of control and craving) begin to take their toll. By now the individual is physically and psychologically addicted to alcohol.

In the early stages, the dynamics and clinical picture of alcoholism vary considerably with each patient and the individual circumstances. In the later stages, the physical, psychological and social deterioration of the alcoholic become entirely too typical. By now alcoholism is truly a disease with a single etiological agent—alcohol—and an essentially unified diagnosis.

A physician treating an alcoholic in the early stages must explore the individual's drinking carefully. Some patients may be able to stop drinking on their own.

Withdrawal symptoms must be anticipated. A good history of the individual's drinking patterns will also help the physician in making the decision whether hospitalization is necessary. If there is reason to expect severe withdrawal symptoms ("the shakes" or even "the dt's"—which appear after two to three days of withdrawing alcohol), the patient should be hospitalized for controlled detoxification with medication. Most units use a combination of drugs (tranquilizers, stimulants, and antidepressants) to try to decrease the severity of withdrawal symptoms. Ideally, the dosage of medication is decreased until, in the last days of detoxification, the patient becomes drug free. Switching from alcohol addiction to other drug addictions and/or combining the two are unfortunately very common.

Antabuse (disulfiram) is often prescribed for patients who have completed detoxification. Antabuse blocks an enzyme which is necessary for metabolizing alcohol in the system and, as a result, the body is oversensitized to alcohol. Thus, when a patient who is taking Antabuse consumes alcohol, highly unpleasant symptoms will develop within a few hours. These may include a sudden drop in blood pressure, cold sweats, palpitations, difficult breathing, a racing pulse, severe headache, and/or reddened skin and bloodshot eyes. Taking a drink, therefore, is negatively reinforced: the alcoholic who is taking Antabuse knows that the consequences of taking a drink will be disagreeable. So he stays dry, no longer ingesting the drug he is physiologically and psychologically addicted to. His functioning improves, if only because of the physiological benefits of sobriety.

Antabuse can be a valuable adjunct to alcoholism therapy. It is not, however, an effective therapeutic agent by itself. It also has side effects in some cases, which may include occasional headaches, skin allergy, fatigue, and loss of sexual potency. Still, it can be useful for an alcoholic who genuinely wants to stop drinking, but is uncertain of his or her ability to maintain sobriety. Ideally, the patient will commit himself to taking Antabuse and will follow through as part of the progress toward recovery.

Medical intervention can be a crucial part of the treatment of alcoholism, but it usually is not effective in itself. So far, no successful pharmacological treatment for alcoholism has been developed. Physiologically, "once an alcoholic, always an alcoholic" holds true. Research on the physiological components of alcoholism, including its possible hereditary factors, plus the anecdotal evidence of the many sobered alcoholics who thought that "just one" wouldn't hurt, all indicate that there is a cluster of biological factors which are only partially amenable to pharmacological therapy. However, if the social and psychological aspects of the alcoholism are successfully treated, the inherent physiological factors do not hamper attaining and maintaining sobriety, all the time the individual does not ingest alcohol.

It is generally agreed that the alcoholic suffers from personality deficits—or inadequate coping mechanisms—that predispose him or her to drink as a means of escaping or seeking gratification through intoxication. Therapy designed to ameliorate these deficits is generally a process of education— teaching the alcoholic to replace inadequate coping mechanisms with healthier ones. Beyond this agreement, as might be expected, views of alcoholism and its therapy vary according to the training of the therapist.

A psychodynamic analyst will see the alcoholic as an emotionally immature, passive dependent individual with strong difficulties in relating meaningfully to others. Alcoholism is a manifestation of "neurosis based on deficient or arrested development of personality, rooted in childhood." Therapy will guide the patient to a search for the introjected experiences from the past that are governing his behavior in the present, interpreting them in a way that guides the patient toward remolding his life. The existential psychiatrist will work with the patient on developing alternative lifestyles which are more gratifying.

The behaviorist sees alcoholism as a "socially acquired, learned behavior maintained by numerous antecedent cues and consequent reinforcers that may be of a psychological, sociological or physiological nature." Therapy will combine

negative conditioning to drinking with positive conditioning to
some alternate lifestyle.

The social psychiatrist will stress the impact of peer groups
on individual behavior. The sociologist may cast the problem as
almost entirely societal, requiring social changes, as does the
activist who discusses "ghetto alcoholism."

Any modern etiology of alcoholism must take into account
the pervasiveness of drinking in our social customs. Like the
peyote of the Yaqui Indian, alcohol has formed part of
mankind's social ritual since prehistory. A complicated ritual
surrounding the use—and sometimes the abuse—of alcohol is
common in human societies. Herodotus reported that one
primitive people routinely debated any issue before the tribe
first sober, then drunk. In the sophistication of upper-class
Edwardian England, an essayist reported:

> We are forever drinking on one excuse or another. A man
> never feels comfortable unless he has a glass before him.
> We drink before meals, and with meals, and after meals.
> We drink when we meet a friend, also when we part from
> a friend . . . We drink the Queen, and the army, and the
> ladies, and everybody else that is drinkable; and I believe
> if the supply ran short we should drink our mothers-in-
> law.

Recognition of the abuses of alcohol and concern with the
relationship of alcoholism to poverty and human degradation
led to an enormous investment in abolishing this drug during
the nineteenth century. But the other side of the coin was also
recognized. The same essayist wrote, for example:

> I can understand the ignorant masses loving to soak
> themselves in drink—oh yes, it's very shocking that they
> should, of course—. . . but think, before you hold up your
> hands in horror, at their ill-living, what "life" for these
> wretched creatures really means. Picture the squalid
> misery of their brutish existence, dragged on from year to
> year in the narrow, noisome room where, huddled like
> vermin in sewers, they welter, and sicken, and sleep . . .

From the hour when they crawl from their comfortless bed
to the hour when they lounge back into it again they
never live one moment of real life . . . In the name of the
God of mercy, let them pour the maddening liquor down
their throats and feel for one brief moment that they live!

In the twentieth century our labeling of the social problems
associated with alcoholism has changed and perhaps improved.
The problems themselves have not. Treatment of alcoholism
must all too often take into account the stresses of poverty,
racism, unemployment and underemployment, and ethnic
discrimination, even though alcoholism is far from confined to
victims of such forces. Therapy will often involve shoring up
depleted supportive systems in the face of difficulties human
beings ought not to have to deal with. "Bandaid therapy," the
political activist sneers, and this charge is undoubtedly accurate.
Nevertheless, in the continuing and marked absence of societal
change, "Bandaid therapy" can still foster change and
improvement in the lives of some.

Alcoholism Therapy
It will be obvious that all the etiological ideas of alcoholism
have some validity, more in some cases than others, depending
on circumstances. By the same token, therapies designed
according to these ideas can be valid, more in some cases than
others, depending on circumstances. There are physiological
factors which render an alcoholic vulnerable to alcoholic
addiction. Alcoholism may well be related to childhood
conflicts, and there is a tendency to reconstruct past behavioral
responses in different environments. Alcoholic behaviors are
"learned" and can be negatively reinforced or extinguished.
Social factors are significant, both the larger forces like poverty
and racism, and the more immediate network of interpersonal
transactions in which the alcoholic lives his life. Behind
alcoholism there is a person, and every alcoholic, like every
person, is different. Or to put this in other words, alcoholism is

the interaction of biological, psychological, and social factors. These factors combine differently, and have different importance, in the life of each individual patient.

The therapist working with alcoholism, therefore, should know as much as possible about alcoholism and its etiology, and take as many individual and social factors as possible into account as a strategy when searching for points of therapeutic entry. Some form of individual or group therapy may be the treatment of choice in one case. In another, work with the problems of alcoholism may be handled by Alcoholics Anonymous while the therapist works with the sobering alcoholic and the family to build a new supportive network. In another case, the therapist may have to help a family cope with the strains of living with an alcoholic who continues to drink. Close consultation with medical personnel may be indicated for a patient who is on Antabuse or other drugs. The more the therapist can deal with the biological, psychological, and social aspects of alcoholism, the more effective therapy can be.

Therapy with Families Affected by Alcoholism

We now turn to the main subject of this book, the discussion of therapy with families affected by alcoholism. Family therapy is only one of many possible therapeutic strategies. Nevertheless, it is often the most effective type of intervention for both primary and preventive therapy. The family is the social unit that is most easily available to the therapist. It is a highly significant, perhaps the most significant, source of the positive and negative feedback that validates an individual's self perception. An alcoholic can maintain his self-perception while recovering with the support of extrafamilial "significant others" like a therapist or A.A. sponsor. But his self-perception while recovering will be greatly enhanced if his competence is positively reinforced by his family group. Finally, the family is a significant source of support to help the individual cope with the demands and stresses of life.

Family therapy of alcoholism is a way of dealing with the needs of the alcoholic in the context of dealing with a human system. *The goal of therapy is not only sobriety. The goal is a changed family*: a system which can support one another as competent human beings.

The basis of family therapy is systems theory. This is a way of looking at human beings which is at once familiar, and yet radically different. Systems theory is based on observations that man undoubtedly made in the cave: people affect each other. If I got caught in a traffic jam on my way into town this morning, and I snarl at your sunny "Good morning," my annoyance will diminish your cheer, just as your cheer will diminish my annoyance. As human beings, we know this to be true. In fact, our experience is so taken for granted that interactional phenomena are often unrecognized.

Systems theory is a way of looking at interaction that makes it available for therapy. Instead of dealing only with John, the alcoholic, we can attack the components of the way John and Mary relate that feed into John's drinking and change those interactions in a way that frees both John and Mary from alcoholic behavior.

Systems theory also gives us a new way of looking at cause and effect in human interaction. Our logical patterns and our very language box us into looking at events in sequences. The idea of causality is grafted onto these sequences: *post hoc, ergo propter hoc.* We say that Mary nags John. In the field of alcoholism, we see the alcoholic as the victim of the family: family stresses add to the alcoholic's anxiety, becoming part of the complex that makes him drink. Or we see the family as the alcoholic's victim: "Years of living with an alcoholic is almost sure to make any wife or child neurotic," advises *Alcoholics Anonymous* "The Big Book" (p. 122). This is a focus which hampers therapeutic interventions. It makes us concentrate on the alcoholic to help him become more coping, *or* focus on helping the family cope with the stresses of living with an alcoholic.

The systems model has a wider focus. Every individual is seen as acting and reacting, in a causal chain that stretches so far back that the idea of cause and effect loses its importance. John had a hard day at work so he came home and bolted two martinis, and when Mary asked shrewishly if he felt better now, he snapped at her. She was hurt, and he felt guilty, because he knew that he was reacting not so much to her nagging as to his hard day, the fact that he sensed he was on his way to another sodden evening, and the fact that he'd promised her and himself yesterday that he'd limit himself to one sherry before dinner . . . Of course, if she didn't nag him, he *would* stop. Only maybe she'd had a hard day too; and it doesn't help when a husband comes home and bolts two martinis . . .

This broader focus seems to be only common sense. It is an attempt (which will always be incomplete) to take more of the components of a syndrome into account. But its effect on therapy is to open whole new fields for possible therapeutic intervention. We still have all the ways of helping John, the individual alcoholic: psychotherapy, behavioral therapy, medical care. But in addition to the focus on the individual, the systems model gives us a way of looking at the context of the alcoholic syndrome and intervening to change it. *The alcoholic is neither victim nor victimizer. His behavior, and the way he thinks and feels, is the result of a whole chain of human interactions. Individual methods of helping the alcoholic have to work with only one link. With the systems model, many other approaches to change become possible.*

Chapter Two

Alcoholism, Family Development and Family Treatment

Definitions of "the family" fill volumes in anthropology, sociology, and psychology. In therapeutic terms, however, a family can be defined rather simply. It is a group of people with a history of life in common. The composition of a family is not the significant factor. A family may be a mother and daughter; or a household composed of two parents, their children, their children's spouses, and the grandchildren; or two lesbians living together with their children; or it may be the "average American" nuclear family. What is significant is that these groups of people have evolved ways of living together, and that these ways of living form a structure which governs the way these people behave and feel.

The easiest way to explore and describe the family in therapeutic terms is to present a paradigm. So let us postulate, following the family therapist Salvador Minuchin, that a family begins when two people join with the purpose of forming a family. This paradigm, as Minuchin points out, is a construct that has as much validity for any individual family as does the "average American family with its 2.2 children." But unlike the average American family, this model gives us a framework for looking at any individual client family against the background of some sort of norm.

Couple Formation: A Paradigm

Let us say that a man and a woman, whom we will call Art and Nancy, have decided to get married. These two individuals have decided to become a couple. A new social group has been delineated..

> *And so, standing before the aforesaid officiator, the two swore that at every other time of their lives till death took them, they would assuredly believe, feel, and desire precisely as they had believed, felt, and desired during the few preceding weeks. What was as remarkable as the undertaking itself was the fact that nobody seemed at all surprised at what they swore. Thomas Hardy: JUDE THE OBSCURE*

The decision to marry (or move in together) is a milestone for Art and Nancy, as for any couple. But their relationship does not spring into being with this decision. Forming a viable dyadic unit is still very much in process. Art and Nancy have been "seeing each other" for six months now. Deeply in love, they are delighted with the process of learning about each other. Art has discovered that Nancy cannot balance her checkbook. He doesn't see this as a problem; in fact, secretly he considers it adorably feminine. He will, of course, manage their combined incomes. Nancy too assumes that Art will handle financial matters; she sees no difficulty with his suggestion that they pool their accounts.

> *It's a pretty story, if you look at it from one point of view; though my wife maintains—and she's a bit of a judge, mind you —that it's not yet finished, she arguing that there's a difference between marrying and being married. You can have a fancy for one, without caring much about the other. Jerome K. Jerome: THE STORY OF HENRY*

Art and Nancy have already begun to learn to tune into each other's feelings and moods. Now this knowledge is expanding.

Art knows that Nancy's department is horrible on Wednesdays, because of the weekly closing. If she snaps at him on Wednesday evening, he teases her about "closingitis." Soon it is accepted between them that Wednesday is a day Nancy doesn't want to have to think about anything but her job.

Art has his moments too, of course. He never loses his temper, but Nancy is learning to listen for a certain edge to his voice, and without realizing it, she tends to leave him alone until the edge disappears.

> . . . when I say in that dangerously thin little voice, "Didn't you think that woman you were talking to for so long at the party tonight was beautiful?" I can count on his saying, "I suppose she was presentable," or "You mean the one with the nose job?" Judith Wax: STARTING AT THE MIDDLE

In the terminology of family therapy, Art and Nancy are developing the transactional patterns which form the structure of the spouse subsystem.

> If she and Rick had had more time it would in the end have been harder. If they had had even a year and then it had happened it would have been harder; if they had had five years, and it had worked out, it would have been desperately hard. And beyond that the old saws did not work, because they worked only on averages and beyond a certain number of years there were no averages. You grew together—and that almost without regard for the quality of your feeling for each other—and you were not as individuals, predictable. Richard Lockridge: PAYOFF FOR THE BANKER

These patterns, often developed with no conscious effort or recognition, operate in ways that become automatic. It is accepted between them that Art is the wit. If Nancy ventures to tell a joke at a party, Art will be slightly startled. His quickly concealed surprise will make Nancy wonder uneasily if she is stealing his thunder, and next time it will be Art who tells the joke.

Some transactional patterns are the result of specific open negotiation, and they are policed by the couple after being attained by discussion and compromise. Both Art and Nancy hate to shop in crowded stores, but Saturday morning is the only time they have. Therefore, Nancy will do the shopping, but Art will drive the car down and pick her up. This is only fair. Other patterns, not specifically negotiated, cannot be rationally agreed on. Art and Nancy both think that husband and wife should share the household drudgery. But Nancy's father, not otherwise a househusband, always took the garbage out. Therefore, Nancy assumes that Art's jobs include emptying the garbage. If he "forgets," she finds herself weeping in a fury of genuine betrayal, to the bewilderment of them both. The issue has become more than the chore. The issue is also Nancy's sense of self and her expectations of herself and Art. Art's and Nancy's conscious and unconscious expectations will have to be worked through and somehow resolved during the long process, which is never entirely finished, of forming a marriage.

One of the couple is an alcoholic in a very early stage. Let us assume it's Art, although it could just as easily be Nancy. Neither Art nor Nancy recognizes Art's drinking as a problem. He gets a little high now and then—who doesn't? Last week he got so drunk at a party that Nancy insisted on driving home, but he'd had an awfully hard day. Nancy's mother jokes that the way to handle a man is to stand at the apartment door with gin and a glass. "As long as it takes him to walk from the elevator to the door, that's how long you pour." Art just loves a good time, that's all. And he wants a wife who'll join him in a life of love and companionship. They'll have fun—enjoy parties and their friends.

When alcoholism appears early in a relationship, denial may also appear from the start. This is very characteristic of families affected by alcoholism. Incipient alcoholics and their spouses are rarely equipped to face the problem. Instead, they try to ignore it. Nancy's tactful "I'll drive, dear," is becoming more and more of a habit. But it's a habit they can live with.

If drinking worsens, however, the necessity of dealing with the problem without acknowledging it complicates unresolved tensions in the relationship. One Saturday morning, Nancy shakes Art awake and tells him she's going shopping; he should meet her in an hour. Three hours later, she finally takes a cab home to find that Art, having tried the hair of the dog for his hangover, is still sleeping it off. Nancy puts all the groceries away by herself and doesn't speak to Art for the rest of the afternoon. By evening things are back to normal, though Art secretly resolves he won't do *that* again, and Nancy silently promises herself that next Saturday she'll make Art drive her down and wait.

As time goes on, drinking influences more and more of the couple's activities. Nancy finds excuses to stay away from family gatherings, because Art got so drunk at Thanksgiving. She stops planning the dinner parties they both enjoyed for the same reason. As his life begins to center more and more on drinking, so does hers. Nancy does the shopping alone now. She also balances the checkbook and, in fact, handles most of the chores. Formerly a meticulous housekeeper, she begins to let things slide. The trash piles up, because that's still Art's job, but that's not the only messy spot in their lives. Art, once also a meticulous housekeeper, hates the way the apartment looks as much as she does, but he's in no position to launch a protest that might start a discussion of what's going on with them.

By now the couple's transactional patterns are organized around the fact that Art's functioning is impaired much of the time. Communications between the spouses have become sparse and ridden with guilt and anger. Negotiating and resolving conflict are hampered because (a) confrontation is contrary to the patterns they have developed and/or (b) "everything would be all right if Art didn't drink so much." In a surprising number of families, however, the problem is never stated that specifically. Many "Arts" and "Nancys" go for years without acknowledging what is happening. A problem that is acknowledged must be dealt with in some way. If Nancy confronted Art with his drinking, he might leave her or she might have to leave him. In any case, she'd have to do *something*, and she has no idea of what to do. She's very angry, and he's very guilty, but there is no way out.

If alcoholism appeared in one spouse's family of origin, that can profoundly affect the formation of the spouse unit. A woman whose father is an alcoholic will probably bring to the marriage the idea that a man cannot manage authority. This becomes part of her expectations of the marital unit. She may hate her father's alcoholism and desire nothing more than to make a new and different life for herself. But she expects men to be relatively passive. Unless this problem can be worked through, a skew in the roles of husband and wife, which will affect the family throughout its existence, may develop.

Nancy doesn't know that her father is an alcoholic. He was never available to her—she can remember long conversations with her mother and very little contact with him. It doesn't occur to her that her mother taught her that the man is the head of the family, while showing her that a man cannot handle that job without the behind-the-scenes management of a loyal wife. Nancy only knows that it seems natural to her to take over the jobs that Art isn't performing, though she resents the drain on her time and energy.

Art, guilty and confused about his own drinking, experiences himself as disqualified by his wife. But it is not his way to confront matters. If he faced the problems that exist, he might have to control his drinking or admit that he can't. In any case, he'd have to do *something*, and he has no idea of what to do.

As everything else in their relationship deteriorates, so does the couple's enjoyment of sex. Nancy has begun to join Art in an evening drink. Sometimes they go out for a walk, which ends in the bar around which Art's social life is more and more centered. When they get home, Nancy goes up to bed. Art sits down to watch TV with a nightcap. Eventually he gropes his way to bed and falls asleep. Sometimes he falls asleep in his chair. Nancy doesn't make an issue of it—that's not her way.

And in a sense, this is a good arrangement for her. Nancy has never truly enjoyed intercourse, and now, with the resentments of the years building up, she would just as soon not sleep with Art. The fact that Art is drinking himself into a stupor most nights takes away from her responsibility for looking at her own sexual desires; his drinking takes her off the hook.

Nancy throws herself into her work. Or has an affair. Or in many cases, begins abusing alcohol herself. Or she goes to a doctor, crying that she's exhausted, that she can't handle everything, that Art drinks too much. The doctor writes a prescription for tranquilizers, and now both spouses float through the evening. In any case, the potential for love, support, and growth within this marriage seems to have evaporated.

For the purposes of illustration, let us now take Art and Nancy to the next step of the family paradigm. Nancy gets pregnant, and they begin to plan for the child.

The child isn't real to Art yet, though he swears that he's going to be a good father. His kids will have everything he never had. Nancy* is planning to switch to part-time work. She'll have a baby and her job—a full life—and do it all magnificently. A nagging unease about Art is pushed aside. Fatherhood will make a new man out of him.

The birth of a baby, however desired and planned for, presents new and urgent problems to any couple. In family therapy terms, the transactional patterns must modify. The spouse subsystem still exists, but there are now also a parental subsystem, a mother-child subsystem, a father-child subsystem, new relationships to the grandparents and extended family, babysitters, the pediatrician, and the other mothers in the park who monitor the infant's development with all the benevolence of Harpies. Or so it seems to Nancy. Nancy feels that she gets scant attention these days. Within a few days, she has gone from "Sit down, honey," to "Nan, the baby's crying!" Art, too,

---

* If Nancy is an alcoholic, fetal damage is a real possibility.

feels aggrieved and neglected. Nan's only working part-time now, so, "for pete's sake why isn't dinner ready?" She hasn't even mixed the martinis, so he mixes the pitcher himself, and pours a little heavily. Later, when Janie is finally asleep, Nancy turns to Art. "I'm going to bed," he mumbles. "Hard day."

In families affected by alcoholism the drinking problem may not have been too much of a strain on spouse transactions. When a family consists only of two adults, an unstructured life is easy to deal with. You don't get up on Saturday because you have a hangover. But both of you sleep till noon, and chores can wait. The birth of a child causes a radical change. Someone must be sober enough to feed the infant and supervise the toddler. In time, supper will have to be served early enough to allow the grade-schooler to do his homework. If there is alcoholism in the family, it will typically have been growing worse during the years of marriage. During the early childhood years, it begins to make a real impact on the family unit.

Now the family must be kept going. And it is the nonalcoholic spouse who has to do it. Sometimes the nonalcoholic spouse collapses into depression, alcoholism, or illness. But in a surprising number of cases, the nonalcoholic spouse does pull himself together, and keeps things going, at least after a fashion. This can go on for years.

In many cases the alcoholic is a wife and mother who doesn't work outside the home. Her alcoholism is relatively easy to conceal. Someone who works outside the home has to be on the job, more or less on time and more or less functional. Progressing alcoholism tends to be picked up relatively early, by the superivsor or co-worker or by the alcoholic himself, who realizes he is not measuring up in the vitally important area of the world of work. A housewife can conceal drinking more successfully. This is a picture that is changing as more and more women join the workforce. But the problem of the "alcoholic housewife" is very much part of the picture of alcoholism.

In our paradigm family, however, the alcoholic is Art. So it is Nancy who takes over. She fathers and mothers the children, and takes on as many of the other family tasks as she can, including keeping up a good front. Art can't possibly work with Little League; he's far too tired on weekends. But she'll be glad to chair the fund-raising committee.

Studies of wives of alcoholics have characterized them as power-driven women who knowingly or subconsciously married an alcoholic because he was a man they could dominate. But this is a view that results from focusing on the problem from the point of view of the individual. When we focus on the alcoholic individual, we see his wife as an adjunct/contributor to the picture. When we look at the couple as a couple, we see the nonalcoholic partner taking on increased executive functioning to compensate for the alcoholic's incapacity. This unquestionably feeds back into the alcoholic's difficulties. It is also true that the alcoholic's difficulties force the nonalcoholic partner to supersede him.

The result in family terms is as unfortunate as the results in individual terms. The alcoholic is pushed to the periphery of the family while the better-functioning family members get on with the business of life. Often he excludes himself, out of guilt. This behavior helps cement an alliance of spouse and children, who blame the alcoholic member for the family unhappiness. Transactional patterns based on compensating for his disability develop. Eventually, any attempt on his part to re-enter will become a threat to the family's structure.

In many families, the children grow up in a conspiracy of silence. Daddy is the head of the family; everyone agrees on that. Mommy does the shopping, the cooking, the bill paying, and in fact most things that get done. Daddy doesn't. So the children learn to help. Daddy is "too tired." And he had "a hard day at work."

> "The poor man can't go . . ." Tess sat up in bed . . , "But somebody must go," she replied. "It is late for the hives already . . ." Mrs. Durbeyfield looked unequal to the emergency. "Some

*young-feller, perhaps would go? One of them who were so much
after dancing with 'ee yesterday," she presently suggested. "Oh
no—I wouldn't have it for the world!" declared Tess proudly.
"And letting everybody know the reason—such a thing to be
ashamed of! I think I could go . . ." Thomas Hardy: TESS OF
THE D'UBERVILLES*

In families affected by alcoholism, the older children
typically take on parental and executive functions rather early.
A first grader comes home afternoon after afternoon to find her
mother "napping" heavily on the couch. She takes her little
brother out of the playpen and minds him until her father
comes home. Then she helps him start dinner. A boy who
finds that his Saturday boat rides with his father get as far as
the boathouse bar eventually elects to stay home, where he
helps his mother with the household chores. The children's
maturity helps stabilize the family. But often this is a psuedo-
maturity, inappropriately assumed at the expense of childhood
developmental tasks.

Children may even become involved in transactions which
ought to be bounded within the spouse subsystem. They group
around the nonalcoholic parent, and while the older son takes
on many of the parenting tasks, the oldest daughter becomes
the housewife. Middle children typically escape from the
family as soon as possible. But smaller children may have to
remain the baby of the family, even when they are well into
their teens. The parent stays close to them, "taking good care of
the children," but also finding a closeness he or she needs in
this relationship.

In family therapy terms, the family has developed a workable
structure that compensates for the inadequacy of a vital family
member. But both spouses lack the support of a spouse
subsystem. The children lack the nurturance and protection of
effective parenting. Everybody lacks the support that would
make it possible to experiment and grow. Janie is 14 now, but
she doesn't date; she has to get dinner and do the dishes. Her
brother Tom doesn't want to join Little League. Even kids

whose parents are divorced bring their fathers to the game. But
he can't ask Art to come or to pitch while he practices batting.

The family is organized around its problem member. Nancy
and the children tacitly blame Art's drinking for all problems,
and they long for his recovery. But a cure would actually be a
threat to the family structure. A sober Art would have to be
allowed to act as husband and father. And such a change would
put the whole family into unexplored territory.

The next developmental stage of the paradigm family is
reached when the children approach adulthood. Now the
children are, or should be, moving out on their own. The
children were the ones who kept the spouses together. (Nancy
has been telling herself for years that she stayed with Art "for
the children's sake.") Now the two spouses are alone again, and
they must again develop a dyadic relationship. At the same
time they must cope with basic changes in their own lives: the
loss of parents, the sense that one's own time is running out,
and perhaps a perceived loss of sexual attractiveness. Many
drinking problems develop or intensify at this stage.

In our paradigm family, Art's drinking has worsened over
the years. Typically, "occasional relief drinking" has turned to
constant, and perhaps surreptitious, drinking. He experiences
memory blackouts and other symptoms of disability which he
cannot ignore. But at the same time that recognition of the
problem can no longer be denied, his dependency on alcohol
increases. By now he is addicted physiologically as well as
psychologically, and persistent remorse and guilt are combined
with grandiose and aggressive behavior. Eventually, physical
deterioration will contribute to the onset of lengthy
intoxications.

All these years Nancy has stood by Art with a Griselda-like
loyalty that is both admirable and destructive. She has called
the office to say he is sick whenever he was too hung over to
make it in. She has stopped seeing family and friends, partly
because it is so much of an effort to keep up appearances, and
partly because she never knows what shape Art will be in. She

has remained loving, protective, and concerned. And her loving acts have fed into the problem, reinforcing Art's incapacity and probably adding to a growing load of resentment and guilt on his part; distress and martyrdom on hers.

The extended family and friends have caught on. The word has sped around the family network, and Art is firmly identified as "a problem." Nancy has confided in a few close friends, and their sympathy buttresses her self-image as the noble martyr. They relate to Art with a sympathy which clearly conveys that he is not quite on an equal footing. Again the problem is not acknowledged, for as long as Art and Nancy don't confront it, it would be very difficult for anyone else in the family to do so. Besides, what could they do?

In the world of work, too, Art's colleagues react with an anxious patience. Alcoholics frequently experience their friends as "acting funny." This is not a paranoid ideation; it is an accurate perception of the friends' attempts to help with the problem without dealing with it directly. The boss, with the best of intentions, takes Art off a challenging assignment and puts him in conditions which will be less stressful for the poor guy. The next morning Art is sick as a pup. His supervisor and closest friend do the estimate he was supposed to work on, give it to him to sign, then send him home to "rest." The bowling team also rallies around. It becomes a regular thing for someone to drive Art home. These are concerned and adaptive responses, but they deprive the alcoholic of validation as a mature, responsible person.

The doctor asked necessary questions; the full name and place of birth and date of birth and so on. Finally Katie asked him a question.

"What are you writing down there—what he died from, I mean."

"Acute alcoholism and pneumonia." . . . *"I don't want you to write down," said Katie slowly and steadily, "that he died from drinking too much. Write that he died of pneumonia alone."*

"Madam, I have to state the entire truth.". . .

"Look," said Katie, "I got two nice children. They're going to grow up to amount to something. It isn't their fault that their father...that he died from what you said. It would mean a lot to me if I could tell them that their father died of pneumonia alone." Betty Smith: A TREE GROWS IN BROOKLYN

The story of this paradigm family can have many endings. When the youngest child enters college, Nancy divorces Art and moves to another city. Or Art leaves the family and drops out of sight. Nancy rears the children, all of them saddened, but also more than a little relieved, to have him gone.

In some cases Art may eventually recover from alcoholism, through individual therapy or perhaps A.A. He and Nancy have grown so far apart that by now this makes little difference to their relationship. But they stay together; where else would Nancy go? By now she is comfortable with the absence of challenge and growth, and she would have no idea of what to do with her life.

For the purposes of this book, however, something brings our paradigm family to the attention of the mental health field. How does a therapist approach a problem like Art and Nancy's? The first step is to identify alcoholism as the major problem and deal with it if necessary.

Often alcoholism is not what brings the family affected by alcoholism to therapy. The patterns of denial still exist. It is not uncommon for members of the helping profession to treat an alcoholic family and never be told about the drinking problem. Truanting, acting out in school, severe depression; many presenting problems may actually relate back to an alcoholism which the family is still denying or concealing.

In general, therapy has two main goals. One is to open the drinking problem to discussion and to therapy if possible. *The alcoholism must be dealt with.* The second is to change the patterns which are keeping these people entrapped in the network of alcoholic-and-participants. If at all possible, the individual should be helped to attain sobriety. But this is only the first step. The sobered alcoholic is still living in social systems organized around his incapacity. For everyone closely involved with an alcoholic, sobriety is a radical change. It may be something they have longed for. But it is a change that will require them to do and see things differently. Nancy, for instance, has gained weight over the years and let her appearance go. Now she can no longer blame her unhappiness on Art's drinking. She is a potentially attractive woman in her late 40's, but she has lost sight of any possibilities other than mother/grandmother and wife of an alcoholic. Now that Art is no longer drinking, what is she to do?

Wherever possible, therapy should focus on the family, changing the patterns that have grown up around the alcoholism, fed by it and feeding into it. Individual therapy often takes these patterns into account in a nonconstructive way, by defining the spouse and family as part of the enemy that the alcoholic has to fight to stay sober. Self-help groups, too, may fail to help the individual learn to act more effectively in the groups in which he lives. It is not at all uncommon for an alcoholic to work intensively with A.A., for his partner to work with Al-Anon, and for both of them to reach a stage where their new individual gains are incompatible with their relationship. A therapy that focuses on changing the family into a network that supports the alcoholic as a sober, functioning member, and that continues to act as a source of support and growth for all family members, is obviously the better strategy.

Therapeutic Implications of the Family Systems Model

This book is not a textbook of family therapy. Its purpose is rather to present cases in which the principles and techniques of family therapy were used to help alcoholic families. Some of the many excellent presentations of theory and technique are listed in the bibliography.

Very briefly, however, family therapy conceptualizes the family as a human social system—a group of humans who develop, in the course of their lives in common, a superstructure which affects the way these individuals behave toward each other and to the world at large.

The family system is organized into subsystems—individuals, generational groups, groups delineated by gender, function, common interest, or simply mutual liking. These units are constantly affecting each other, and any change in one unit will affect all the others to a greater or lesser degree.

The family system exists within other systems made up of the extended family, the community, the region, the country, and the immediate world. Society demands certain tasks from the family, and changes in society require changes in the family. At the same time, the family must maintain continuity —it has the main responsibility for giving individuals a sense of belonging—a sense of where they "come from."

The interphases of all subsystems, from the individual/individual up to the nation/world are called boundaries. The function of a boundary is to delineate the group, while giving it access to information from other groups. A boundary must separate and protect; it must also unite and give access. Much of the work of family therapy focuses on these boundaries within the family, exploring and modifying the way a husband (an individual subsystem) relates to his wife, the way the spouse subsystem relates to the sibling subsystem, and so on.

An individual is a subsystem of the family as well as a person in her own right. If our focus is an individual alcoholic, and we change her, we will also change her family, whether intentionally or not. In family therapy, the focus will be changing the network of family relationship forces, rather than the alcoholic member alone. In many cases the therapeutic target will be a dyad, triad, or larger relationship's interactions.

Therapy with families affected by alcoholism has two major foci. One is combating the problems posed by alcoholism. The other is to help this individual family attain the best functioning possible for it. This requires knowledge beyond expertise in alcoholism and family functioning. The therapist must also take the family's ethnic background into account. Strengthening the boundaries around the nuclear family is probably an incorrect approach to the problems of an Italian-American family whose grandmother is accepted as the matriarch. The family's developmental stage should also be considered in the therapeutic approach. The goal may be to help a sobered father learn to take on parental functions. If he is dealing with a young child, the emphasis will be on nurturance and guidance. If he is dealing with an adolescent, the therapist will have to help the father learn to negotiate, maintaining the authority of a parent while remaining flexible enough to allow the adolescent to grow and separate.

This is the value the family paradigm has to a therapist. It gives the therapist not only a way of looking at a client family, but also a direction for therapy. It can also help separate the significant from the unimportant. A therapist might have problems working with a family whose parents beat the children as a method of discipline. But since the therapeutic goal is to help the parents assert their parental authority, the therapist can focus correctly on rewarding this parental assertion, rather than attacking the method used. These general principles will be illustrated again and again in the case examples that follow. Therefore, let us take the plunge and consider how therapy can be initiated with an alcoholic or a family affected by alcoholism.

The first family interview is a time for assessing each member's position in the family. Having attained a working diagnosis of this family's structure, the therapist will then start working to move each family member in a way that begins correcting the structural skews caused by alcoholism.

The problem of alcoholism itself will have to be acknowledged and sometimes dealt with. In some families this is easy; alcoholism is the presenting problem. Giuseppi mentioned his drinking in the phone call making the appointment for the first interview. He said he had been a heavy drinker for almost twenty years, before stopping one and one-half years ago. Now he was drinking again, and he felt himself slipping into old patterns. A family interview was arranged, in which Giuseppi's drinking was the first order of business.

Ian sought therapy for marital problems. He said he wanted to explore his relationship with his wife, to keep the family together. In the first session he talked almost exclusively about his relationship with his wife. She was neglecting herself and had stopped trying to attract him sexually. He'd entered some extramarital relationships as a method of seeking sexual gratification.

Only when he was saying goodbye did he casually mention, "By the way, I probably should tell you that I think I have a drinking problem." The therapist shared with him that she had picked that up during the session. His eyes were very red, his face was swollen, and although he was not a heavy man, he had a large stomach. The therapist told him she thought they would have to talk about this and made an appointment for the next day to focus on Ian's drinking. Alcoholism was affecting his work and his relationship with his children, to say nothing of his marriage. Unquestionably it was a serious problem, affecting not only the spouse, but also the whole family.

Riva also presented her problem as a marital conflict. While the therapist was talking to her, it became clear that these marital problems were related to her husband's drinking. Through her seeking therapy, her husband and daughter were brought into treatment that dealt with her husband's drinking, as well as what it had done to the family.

In other cases alcoholism, even of long duration, is deliberately concealed. Mary, a twenty-year-old divorcee and mother of a two-year-old daughter, came to therapy after hospitalization for severe depression. She had been abusing drugs for years, but was not using them when she entered the psychiatric ward. After admission, she became completely withdrawn. A family session was arranged with the participation of Mary, her baby, and her parents, with whom

Mary was again living. As the session progressed and it became apparent that Mary insisted on remaining mute, the therapist decided to split the family group by sending the father out to an adjacent room where he could observe his wife and daughter through a one-way mirror.

The therapist's purpose was to see if the mother and daughter could open up in the father's absence. But when the cotherapist sat beside Mr. McCarthy behind the mirror, she was struck by the strong smell of alcohol on his breath, though it was only 9:15 a.m. She asked Mr. McCarthy to rejoin his family and immediately confronted him, "Were you drinking before the session?"

Now that the problem was out in the open, Mary suddenly began to talk. She spoke of her own experiences with alcohol and her strong resentment toward her father for having used her as a drinking partner while she was in her early teens. At this point the focus changed from a depressed, uncooperative young adult to the alcoholism in the family which had been covered up by all the family members for years.

In the Giacomelli family the mother, Anina, was an alcoholic. But again, the entire family concealed the problem. The family came into therapy after the father called a mental health center to request help for Anina. But he reported only that she was suffering from severe depression.

Anina herself believed that no one knew of her drinking. She disguised her frequent periods of incapacity as headaches, and everyone in the family, extended family, neighborhood, and church politely maintained this fiction. In the first family session, however, the therapist picked up some clues that Anina might have a drinking problem. Only in her thirties, Anina looked like a woman in her fifties. She was overweight, her eyes were red, and her face was suspiciously puffy. The therapist began to explore with the family what Anina's life was like. The youngest child, Julian, 8, let the cat out of the bag, and within minutes the entire family was sharing their feelings about Anina's drinking. Shocked by the realization that everyone not only knew of her drinking but hated it, Anina attempted suicide. She had to be rushed to the emergency room. But therapy, which began again as soon as possible, could now focus both on the drinking and on the family problems it created.

Whether alcoholism is acknowledged or uncovered during the course of therapy, the family therapist must establish a therapeutic contract with the entire family plus the alcoholic member. It must be understood that therapy will deal with the drinking problem *and* with the problems of the entire family. Ideally, work on sobriety can be done while family problems are attacked in a mutually reinforcing multimodal strategy.

It is often desirable to hold individual sessions with the alcoholic concurrently with early family sessions. In these individual sessions, the therapist can get a good history to determine the stage of the alcoholism. Medical referrals may be desirable. Ego strengths in the alcoholic can be picked up and built up, and any accomplishment can be praised and reinforced to increase self-esteem. Close, perhaps daily, contact may be necessary. The therapist may set a time for daily phone contact which maintains communication, supports the alcoholic, and also begins the process of helping the alcoholic establish a routine for his or her life.

Alcoholics Anonymous can be very useful here. The contact with people who have experienced what he is experiencing is invaluable to the patient, as is the support of the group. Furthermore, A.A. can be continually available, as a therapist cannot be, and its members know how to deal with those crisis situations which the patient has not yet learned to cope with.

Individual sessions with the alcoholic plus the participation of A.A. make it possible to de-emphasize the drinking problem in the family sessions. Teaching the family about alcoholism is often an important step. They must learn that alcoholism is an illness and to adjust to it as they would to any other chronic illness in a family member. But they must also learn not to blame alcoholism for all problems which arise. The therapist must point out that the individual alcoholic is working on his or her drinking. Individual work will be done with other family members, if necessary, and/or they may be referred to Al-Anon or Alateen. But the goal of therapy is a better functioning family unit.

In the process, the therapist will work with the spouses on the spouse relationship. There will be sessions with them centering on their roles as parents. There will be sessions with the children, helping them turn over the parental and executive roles they have inappropriately assumed and helping them find compensations for this change in age-appropriate ways. The goal is a viable foundation from which the family can grow.

The Williams

Helping the alcoholic attain sobriety is not enough. This is shown by the many cases in which families continue growth-hampering family patterns even though drinking behavior has disappeared.

The Williams family was a case in which both parents were alcoholics with a twenty-year history of problem drinking. The spouses had separated for four years, during which each had worked individually on his own drinking problems through A.A. and treatment with different individual therapists. Finally, they had reconciled for the sake of their children. At this point Paul had been sober for a year and a half, and Janet for eight months. But sobriety was not enough. The couple felt unable to integrate their individual growth into their relationship as husband and wife, and this difficulty was hampering their individual work. Janet felt she needed a man in the house to be her co-parent, but she did not want to relate to Paul sexually or to fulfill his other demands as a husband in a relationship that did not include drinking. She simply didn't know Paul as a sober man. But both Janet and Paul were willing to work at becoming better parents. Consequently, a family session was arranged. Probably they both, at this stage, felt much more comfortable working as parents, rather than focusing on marital problems.

Whatever the individual problem or presenting problem may be, the entire family becomes the patient. In the first session, therefore, both parents and children were present, and the therapist began to assess the family's existing structure. The younger children, Jean, 13, and Bob, 11, complained in the session that their brother Fred, 18, bossed them around. The therapist inferred that Fred had become the substitute father for the younger children. Thus one treatment goal was immediately obvious; to help Fred step down from his role as substitute father, while helping Paul reestablish himself as the father. This was not conveyed to the family, but the therapist mentally formulated three steps toward that goal. The family would have (1) to recognize the existing family structure, which included Fred's dysfunctional displacement of his father, (2) to see that displacement as undesirable, (3) to understand that this confusion of roles was the result of a long period of parental drinking, but that the parents were now capable of acting as parents.

The therapist raised the subject of alcoholism and how it had affected the family. Everyone denied that this had ever been a problem. Fred, who often acted as family spokesman, said, "You have the wrong idea. There was never any lack of food in the house." The therapist persisted, asking who took care of the household chores, like cleaning. Paul Jr., 15, grimaced and pointed to himself. This was another example of a child's stepping into an executive role as a direct consequence of the behavior of alcoholic parents. While drinking, they had in effect become absent members of the family.

As the session continued, the position of each member of the family became clearer. Fred was a parental child, whose authoritarian behavior had been supported by his mother. Paul Jr., who had assumed some of his mother's tasks in doing the household chores, was referred to by her as the good boy of the family. The two youngest children were withdrawn, but seemed much younger than their age. Jean, at 13, had closed off communication with her family in order to avoid their overwhelming expectations. Her older sister had taken care of the whole family before marrying at the age of 17, perhaps as a way of opting out of the family conflicts. Everyone compared Jean to that sister, urging her to be neater and more diligent. Bob, at 11, used baby talk. Throughout the session, the mother corrected the children's behavior, telling them to speak up or sit straight, remarking, "You should have washed your hands before we got here," or "tied your shoes," and so on. It seemed obvious that Janet babied the children, probably so she could keep herself busy in the role of a mother with young children who needed constant attention.

The father was an outsider, only now beginning to relate to his family, but doing so mostly as a disciplinarian. His attempts to be a good father were sincere, but his contact with his children tended to be confined to lecturing.

The first session was largely exploratory. But at its end, Paul, Sr., pointed out that this was the first time in years the family had been able "to sit together and talk without yelling and screaming." The family left the session with a feeling of hope. Lines of communication had been reopened. The two parental children were beginning to realize that their parental functioning was inappropriate because no longer necessary, and the parents were recognizing that their drinking had pushed the children into roles from which they now needed to be freed.

The therapeutic goal with the Williams family was to change the interactions that kept the children in executive positions and the parents as incompetents. In particular, Paul Jr. and Fred would have to return executive authority to their parents and find developmentally appropriate compensations for this ceding of power.

To accomplish this, Paul and Janet would have to learn to support each other as parents. One approach to this problem was spouse sessions in which the therapist encouraged the couple to work on their relationship. Part of the problem was Paul's long and irregular working hours. Supported by the therapist and by Janet's statement that she needed him at home, Paul was able to confront his boss and tell him he would no longer be available for unlimited overtime. Fortunately, Paul had already reached a point in his recovery where he didn't have to compensate by proving to himself that he was a good provider.

As Paul began to spend more time with his family, he was able to practice supportive ways of acting as a husband and father. Naturally this change did not come easily. The homeostatic mechanisms that keep a family functioning in its usual manner have great power. For example, when Janet and Paul were drinking, the family had had no regular mealtimes. One of the things the couple wanted to establish as a ritual symbolizing their new life was a regular dinner hour. But almost every night one of the children was late. Still, the improvement in the spouse relationship was supporting change. Janet was learning to express anger openly, instead of covertly punishing Paul by rejecting him sexually. Gradually the couple were working their way toward mutual support as they resumed their roles as parents.

Bob was the first to react visibly to this family change. He had been very close to his mother, often even sleeping in her bed. When his father came home, he felt displaced. To him, the improving relationship between his parents meant loss, and he ran away.

Once Paul and Janet would have used alcohol to alleviate the anxiety caused by such a crisis, and they would have acted independently instead of as a parental team, contradicting each other and increasing the confusion until one of the older children stepped into the vacuum. This time, Paul was at work when Janet learned that Bob had run away. She turned to her A.A. sponsor; as she later explained, she wanted to be sure of getting support, and didn't feel her relationship with Paul was strong enough for her to lean on him. She was afraid that this stressful situation might jeopardize her sobriety; if unsupported, she might regress to her old pattern of drinking to resolve problems.

The therapist framed this crisis as an opportunity for Paul and Janet to practice problem-solving together. An emergency session was arranged with the couple so they could discuss how they would deal with Bob when he returned.

For perhaps the first time in this couple's relationship, they were able to sit down together and make decisions about their children's problems. The therapist encouraged them to support each other without blaming themselves for the incident.

Alcoholics should not be pushed to take responsibility too soon. Experimenting with a new way of living, they have to learn to trust themselves and the people around them. In this situation Janet, feeling the need of support, had turned to her A.A. sponsor instead of calling her husband. Paul was wounded, but after discussing the present state of their relationship with the therapist, he was able to accept Janet's fear of being let down by him. Thus the situation posed an opportunity not only for better functioning as parents, but also for further progress in the spouse subunit.

Paul's reaction to Bob's running away had been rage. In the session with the spouses, the therapist helped him calm down and understand the dynamics of the incident. By running away, Bob was giving his family a message which he could not verbalize. Together, therapist and parents set a therapeutic goal. When Bob came back, they would help him verbalize his reasons for leaving home. The couple left the session feeling united and ready to deal with their son.

Bob was found in the evening, and a session was immediately arranged for the following morning. At the beginning of the session Bob was unable to talk, but after a while, with the help of the therapist and both his parents, he was able to say, "I had to go. There isn't enough room in the house for Daddy and me." The mood of the session changed; everybody was shocked, including the therapist. Paul's hurt was obvious on his face.

Everyone was silent for a few moments. Then Janet, facing Bob with a lot of difficulty, managed to say, "I need both of you. I care for both of you." This statement, coming on the heels of rejection by both his wife and son, brought tears to Paul's eyes. Watching his rigid father showing feeling and listening to his mother, Bob saw, for perhaps the first time in his life, that his parents were responsible and caring adults to whom he could talk. Everyone agreed that Bob must be helped to talk to his parents. The therapist also promised to alert Bob's Alateen sponsor, to help Bob find age-appropriate peer-group compensations for the necessary distancing from his mother.

Bob's difficulty talking to his parents was another direct result of their alcoholism. Children cannot experience a drunk adult as a rational, approachable, possible guide to the child's problems in growing up. This therapeutic session may well have been Bob's first opportunity to talk to his mother and father. He, like the other children, would have to learn that his parents were no longer incompetents to be protected, but responsible adults who could help and guide them.

Later in therapy, the focus shifted to Fred, who was (the younger children reported) drinking and smoking far too much. It is unfortunately common to find the children of alcoholics becoming alcoholics themselves. But the family focus in this case made preventive work possible. The fact that alcoholism was now discussed openly allowed Paul and Janet to share some of their own experiences with drinking when they were teenagers. Because his parents were able to share the memory of their emotions directly, these discussions had a profound effect on Fred.

The therapist urged the family to role-play a family scene in which drinking behavior had been present. This proved quite useful in helping the children share what they had experienced during the years when their parents were drinking and in making the parents realize the impact their behavior had had on their children.

At the same time, the Williams family had to learn to detach from alcoholism. When old behaviors were used and blamed on the time the parents were actively drinking, the therapist made the family aware that the alcoholism was not there any more. The problem must be dealt with in new terms. Specifically, Janet and Paul had to learn to support each other without blaming and to make demands on each other without the fear that making demands would drive the partner back to drinking. The children also had to learn to stop protecting both parents for fear of making them resume drinking.

After seven months of therapy, the Williams family decided to stop treatment. Paul and Janet were maintaining sobriety, and the family members all agreed that they felt comfortable with the changes that were happening. The therapist agreed with them, but impressed on them the fact that help would always be available if the family felt unable to cope with further changes, including the normal changes that are part of every family's growth.

The treatment of the Williams family demonstrates many of the components of treating families affected by alcoholism. Alcoholism has a profound effect on a family network, which must organize to compensate for the alcoholic's incapacity. Recovery from alcoholism is only a first step to the achievement of health for the system. The effectiveness of therapy can be maximal only if the social components of alcoholism and its consequences are corrected.

The Fitzpatricks

Alcoholics often have genuine difficulty in recognizing anything abnormal about their behavior, particularly when their denial has persisted over a period of years. To this type of alcoholic, everyone else acts funny, or worse. Sometimes this perception that others need help can be used to bring the alcoholic to therapy.

I first met Pat Fitzpatrick at a group meeting on an alcoholism detoxification ward. Many such units hold daily group meetings in order to give an opportunity for ventilating feelings and/or for treatment. Meetings generally begin with complaints about the director, the nurse, the recreational facilities, and the food. Unhappiness is projected to the current environment. But in the process, the subject of alcohol use or abuse is brought up. Stories designed to elicit the group's sympathy are told, and the group usually responds profusely. In this supportive atmosphere others begin to share their own unhappiness, and without the group's awareness, the meeting becomes first educational and then motivational. In the discussion of very personal complaints, participants may begin to think about what they could do for treatment.

One day there was a new man in this particular group. He sat morosely in the corner, one eye blackened and one arm in a sling. It was Monday morning, rarely the happiest part of anyone's week, and the men gathering were grumbling more than usual as they sat down. Everyone seemed glum—restless after the weekend, with its decreased staff and curtailed activities. The griping became general.

Suddenly some remark seemed to touch a nerve in Pat. He sat up and began a bitter complaint about his wife. *She* was the crazy one. She should be locked up, not he.

The other men listened sympathetically as Pat protested the injustice of being committed by his crazy wife just because he'd been beaten up in a bar. The group urged Pat to see that his wife got help. Everyone agreed that, "Crazy people have to be cared for."

The group's support was crucial to Pat's willingness to enter therapy. The peer group helped him conceive therapy as a step to help his wife.

Hospital procedure required that Pat be psychiatrically evaluated. He cooperated, continuing to insist that his wife was the crazy one. The psychiatrist recommended he join his wife in therapy, for her sake. This coming on top of the group's discussion helped him accept therapy.

> *"Gaolbird! Monster! . . . Where's the money? What have you got in your pockets?—show me!" . . . There was not a single kopek. "Where is the money, then?" she cried. "Oh, God, he can't have drunk it all! There were twelve silver roubles left in my box! . . ."*
> Feodor Dostoevsky: CRIME AND PUNISHMENT

We had learned that Pat, 43, lived with Mary, 41, and their daughter Gina, 22, who had recently moved back with her parents after breaking up with her boyfriend. When I got in touch with Mary to arrange the first appointment, she stated angrily that she had committed Pat to a hospital specializing in alcoholism for two weeks' treatment and observation. "This time was the last straw," she said.

Questioning gently, I learned that Pat had been unemployed for months. Mary conceded that he did some of the household chores, but she seemed to see him as a bum living off his wife's and daughter's earnings. A few weeks ago, the family had decided to buy a used car; they all missed having one. Their credit rating was poor and they had no checking account, but Mary and Gina had scraped together $1,000 in cash and given it to Pat so he could choose the car. Pat had started out that morning with the cash and the best of intentions. But on his way to the auto dealer's, at 9 a.m., he'd apparently decided to stop for a drink. Around three that afternoon the police had called Mary at work to tell her that Pat, heavily intoxicated, had been beaten up in the bar and required medical attention. Mary had found her husband with a black eye and a dislocated shoulder, and without the $1,000, for which he was totally unable to account. Furious, Mary committed him to the detoxification unit of a center specializing in alcoholism.

Mary said she was at the end of her rope. She only hoped the doctors would "straighten him out." But when I asked her to come to the hospital for a session and bring Gina, she readily agreed.

The psychiatric resident asked me to join him as a cotherapist. This was taking a risk, because we did not know each other. But having met Pat on the ward and talked with Mary, I agreed to give it a try. To establish a closer cotherapist relationship, we agreed to meet before and after the session to establish therapeutic goals and to evaluate the transactions. Our earliest formulation was that as a therapeutic team, we could model a couple negotiating conflicts for Pat and Mary.

Mary was a short, scrawny, plainly dressed woman with a sour expression. Gina's face was attractive, but she looked more like a fifteen-year-old than a college graduate. She was dressed like a teenager and was extremely shy. As soon as they entered the room Mary and Gina sat down close to each other. Pat sat on the opposite side of the room close to the therapists, a spatial arrangement that turned out to be a very good picture of the family's organization.

Mary immediately began to rail at Pat. Words could not express the life she'd led with this drunkard. The loss of all that money had only capped years of suffering. She demanded that the therapists make Pat "do something" about his drinking. Gina said nothing, but she grasped Mary's hand and glared at her father.

Pat did not remember the loss of the money, either because of a blackout or because his denial was so strong. He was totally bewildered by Mary's attack. Then he became furious. He still felt that Mary had violated his personal rights by committing him, and accusations flew back and forth. The couple was locked into an exchange of charges and countercharges which had virtually closed off any other aspect of their lives.

Gina watched her shouting parents anxiously. The therapists guessed that Gina, having broken up with her boyfriend, now felt trapped between her parents and roped into their problems. Each of the family members seemed at once overinvolved and estranged from the others. The two women needed help just as much as Pat did.

The therapists interrupted the marital quarrel to focus the session on plans for Pat's discharge from the hospital. This often turns out to be a helpful perspective. The technique makes the family look at an alcoholic as a sick person involved in a recovery process. There is hope of change, but also recognition that change will not come overnight, any more than recovery from any other serious illness. This task helps the family unite around a real issue.

Pat's physician had recommended Antabuse. Mary leapt on that point, insisting that Pat accept the prescription. That insurance that he would stop drinking was very important to her. Pat resisted, partly because of Mary's diatribe, and partly because to him, taking Antabuse was a sign of weakness—that he wasn't man enough to handle his recovery. The therapists helped the couple negotiate a compromise. Pat would take the Antabuse, but Mary would not nag him about it, check up on him, or complain about his meeting his buddies at the neighborhood bar. This agreement was an important first step in rebuilding their relationship.

By the end of the first session several desirable therapeutic goals for this family became clear. An obvious one was alcoholism education. The Fitzpatricks had been living with the problems of alcoholism for twenty years, but didn't understand them or the emotional stress of living in an alcoholic situation. The therapists would have to help them conceive of alcoholism as an illness, to see how this illness affected their lives, and to learn to deal with it. The second goal would be rebuilding the marriage. Pat and Mary seemed to want to stay together, but they would have to work on their relationship. This would be important, too, for the third goal: to set Gina free from the triad.

Gina was a troubled young woman. She couldn't identify with her mother—a dissatisfied, bitter woman, or with her father—an alcoholic unable to be father or husband. At the same time, she was badly overinvolved in her parents' lives. She had experienced living on her own, but she had come home to save the family. Now that things were so bad at home, she couldn't leave. Obviously, she was in a trap.

The therapists and family agreed that Pat would enter group therapy, with the specific goal of working on his sobriety. Pat and Mary resisted the idea of A.A. and Al-Anon ("It's *his* problem," Mary snapped), but Pat felt comfortable with the idea of group therapy. In addition, the threesome would continue in family therapy, and there would be several sessions with Pat and Mary alone, to focus on marital issues.

Pat kept his commitment to take Antabuse and work on his drinking problem. Mary kept her end of the bargain, and as Pat's functioning improved, so did their marriage. His improving health also had important ramifications in their extended family. The Fitzpatricks lived in the same house with

Mary's parents, who occupied the first floor, with her sister and brother-in-law on the floor above. This arrangement, not uncommon in ethnic groups where the importance of the extended family is simply taken for granted, meant that Pat was up against a formidable array of Italian in-laws with a family bias against the Irish. As Pat's problems developed, Mary's mother had repeatedly told her, "We warned you not to marry that bum." Gradually Mary withdrew from her family because of the shame of Pat's drinking. Pat's family, much more accepting of drinking, tended to blame Mary for his problems. Thus, Pat's improvement made it possible for the couple to reestablish some sorely missed ties to both sides.

As family sessions proceeded, Pat, Mary and Gina started to accept alcoholism as an illness, not a weakness, and their individual problems as family problems, not just as Pat's drinking. Next, we addressed ourselves to specific steps designed to help Gina separate from her parents' conflicts. She had a good job, and with the therapists' encouragement and the reassurance of her parents that they could take care of themselves, she made plans to move to her own apartment. Pat and Mary, now very aware of having overinvolved Gina in their lives, were careful to let her know that they would take care of their own problems in the future, if necessary seeking further couples' therapy.

During this period, we held several sessions with Pat and Mary alone, to discuss what they wanted in a husband-wife relationship. They began to work out some of the resentments of the past and in the process build a new relationship which compensated for the vacuum created by Gina's leaving.

After three months, Gina had moved to her own apartment and bought her own car. She had returned to graduate school and was dating a new boyfriend. Mary was beginning to depend on Pat, and he was able to give warmth and support and accept it from her. They were developing outside activities which both enjoyed very much, so they no longer needed Gina as a daily part of their lives. We could see the change even in Mary's appearance.

At the end of six months the psychiatric resident left the hospital staff. A session was scheduled to discuss this development and Gina was also invited. The therapists hardly recognized her. She was dressed like a woman her age, with a new hairstyle which set off her beautiful face. When the issue of continuing the sessions was brought up, Pat and Mary opted to terminate therapy. Pat was to continue in group therapy, and the couple felt they could integrate progress with their marriage without further help.

During this period the Fitzpatricks had acquired tools they had never known to help them work with conflict and face problems in their family life in a more healthy way. We had the impression that we had opened a door, and that these three people could now let themselves become part of the outside world.

The O'Briens

A young adult alcoholic can sometimes be expressing his family's pathology by drinking. This case illustrates the life of one such man, who started individual treatment for alcoholism. The family was seen for a few exploratory sessions, but family treatment proved unsuitable, and individual therapy continued as the treatment of choice.

Jack, 19, was the older son of John and Alice O'Brien. John was a successful lawyer, and Alice was a teacher. Both functioned well in their professional lives. The younger son, Peter, was a high school student.

Now in college, Jack was having serious problems with excessive drinking. Concerned about the situation, Alice called an outpatient clinic that specialized in the treatment of alcoholism and made an appointment for her son. Jack met the therapist—a man not much older than himself—and developed a good relationship with him.

. . . for at least half an hour I studied the grain on the bartop and learned therefrom a great deal about the structure and purpose of the Universe; I leaped up on that same bartop and performed a

*hornpipe—on my hands. After that it all got a bit vague and
hallucinatory . . . Spider Robinson: "PYOTR'S STORY"*

Jack had had his first drink at the age of 9, when his father
took him to a bar to reward him for good grades in school. At
13, he began drinking heavily and by now was consuming a
pint of whiskey and twelve cans of beer almost daily. Jack's
mother called him schizophrenic; his father called him crazy;
and his job supervisor at the college library said he was an
imbecile. Jack had always been taunted in the neighborhood,
labeled "queer" and "weirdo." He wanted to be a writer, but
said he could write only when drunk.

After evaluation, Jack decided to continue with the treatment
offered, which implied a decision to stop drinking. The
therapist suggested Antabuse as an adjunct to therapy, and Jack
agreed to take it.

As soon as he stopped drinking, his functioning began to
improve. Encouraged, the therapist decided to engage the
family in treatment with the hope that this would accelerate
Jack's recovery. Jack agreed somewhat reluctantly, and
arrangements were made to have the whole family come to the
agency. The therapist asked me to join him in a few
exploratory family sessions as a consultant.

John O'Brien arrived at the agency at the set time, but Jack
and his mother were twenty minutes late. They apologized,
saying they'd had trouble driving in the snow. Alice O'Brien
immediately said that Peter was not coming since he had to
attend some after-school activity.

As they were taking seats in the small room assigned for the
session, the family plunged into a discussion of Jack's drinking.
This was no surprise to the therapists; almost invariably,
alcoholism plays a central role in a family and their exchanges.
However, experience with alcoholism does not necessarily teach
people the facts about the problem, or the way to deal with it.
Both parents were rambling, mumbling abstractly about how
destructive "drinking can be." Nothing positive was mentioned
about Jack's accomplishment, or his five months of sobriety. As

in many families affected by alcoholism, Jack's problem was a scapegoat used to avoid discussing other problems in the family.

Jack became upset and complained that his parents were lecturing again. At home his mother talked about his drinking all day long, and he hated it.

Strange as it may sound, Alice had arranged a party in the neighborhood pub to celebrate Jack's coming birthday. However, when Jack said he would like to have a mug of beer on his birthday, a family squabble developed. Alice O'Brien was clearly sending a double message: "You shouldn't, but you can."

The subject was dropped when John began to request information on how long the desire to drink persists in recovering alcoholics. Before the therapists could answer the office phone rang. It was Peter, asking to speak to his mother or father immediately. Alice picked up the phone, listened, and said she couldn't attend to him now because she was involved in the session. She asked him why he had said he would be too busy to come to the session, if he was home already. Then we heard her resisting Peter's request to speak to John, though she finally acquiesced and handed the receiver to her husband. John spoke abruptly to him and said he could not spend time on the phone now and hung up. Mother and Jack were watching and listening attentively.

When John hung up Jack said tearfully that Peter's excuse was not true. He just didn't want to become involved; he didn't care about Jack's therapy. Alice defended Peter, stating angrily that Peter had always been concerned about Jack. Hadn't he taken an active role in throwing away Jack's whiskey as well as insisting on the importance of getting Jack into treatment? Peter, she said, had suffered so much, the poor boy, and *he* had never made her run to the neighbors, "hat in hand." Jack was overwhelmed with fury.

Alice continued defending Peter. John interrupted, as if totally unaware of Jack's reaction, to comment cheerfully on

Peter's "Freudian reaction formations" in his manner of showing love toward Jack.

The therapists, responding to Jack's anger, tried to stop both parents and make them aware of him. Jack was raging, demanding that his mother talk about "hat in hand." For the last few days, he said, he'd been thinking about taking a drink, just to show his family.

This was a crucial element to understanding the dislocation of thinking in the family system. It seemed that even extreme anger bounced off Jack's parents. Only his drinking attracted their attention.

Alice began to talk about Jack's problems as a child with a voice devoid of emotion. She said that he had been hyperactive. She had studied, reading everything related to Jack's condition that was then available. John shrugged and sat back, tuning out his wife's monologue. Jack calmed down until Alice got off the track and began talking about Peter and how she became so absorbed working with Jack that Peter was ignored.

Jack grew increasingly upset as she talked about his brother. He began to complain about Peter, saying he was constantly terrorized by him. Jack said he could never get his own way when Peter was around. Mr. O'Brien sat up straight and supported Jack, saying that Alice always defended Peter even in the worst aspects of his behavior. Father seemed to be strongly allied with Jack; in fact, he was fighting his wife through Jack.

Feeling supported, Jack began to give examples of how his brother terrorized him. He said Peter used to change channels when he was watching a TV program. Alice ignored his complaints and said that Peter had lacked experiences in life, whereas Jack had had everything—even a trip to Europe. In fact, Jack was now dating the girl who had been Peter's girlfriend. She continued on the same track talking about Peter's deprivations.

Suddenly Jack exploded, screaming furiously that he wanted his mother to tell us about this "hat in hand." Everything always revolved around Peter, he complained. Even now she was getting off the track, talking about Peter. He was sick of it.

Alice was startled and said she didn't know what Jack wanted. The exchange continued, Jack demanding that his mother go on with the "hat in hand" business and Alice feigning no knowledge of it. Finally, when Jack persisted, she explained to the therapists that the expression referred to the time when the parents in the neighborhood had contacted her, complaining that Jack was involved in an adolescent homosexual situation. She'd had to go running, "hat in hand" she said, to defend him. The question arose: Had Jack been in difficulty even before his drinking started?

John joined Jack and intimated for the first time that his wife didn't allow him to act as a father to Peter. Jack screamed that he resented all the talk about Peter. Alice resumed her narrative about her struggles to raise Jack. At that point, John said that Jack had been brutalized as a young child in school because of his eccentric behavior and his interest in stamps. This engaged him in a fight with the school administration on his son's behalf.

The open alliance between John and Jack may have been too much for Alice. She drew the therapists' attention to herself, saying that she had something painful she wanted to say. She often felt, she said, that she had three sons. Her husband always came to her to make decisions about the boys. He complained about Peter to her, instead of dealing with his son himself.

Alice's behavior at this point was a repetition of a family pattern the therapists had noted before. Whenever one member of this family began to relate to another—John defending Jack, in this case—a third member entered, interrupting the first two by bringing up different problems.

Now Alice continued her complaints. When Peter was born, she said, John said he felt he had just gained a "brother." John, somewhat embarrassed, growled, "What's wrong with that?"

Alice answered that she felt dissatisfied as a woman. John retorted defensively that he felt dissatisfied as a man.

The focus of the session seemed to be veering toward the couple. They began attacking each other, but Jack interrupted, not allowing his parents to interact. Again the pattern of this family emerged: a dyadic (dual) interchange generally interrupted by the entrance of a third.

Since the agency allowed no flexibility in scheduling, the session had to end at this point. The therapists felt overwhelmed by the mass of information and the chaotic way this family communicated. But they encouraged the family to return for another session, and they agreed.

John, Alice and Jack arrived together for the second session. Peter was not with them, and again Alice explained apologetically that Peter was not coming. This had been a shock, she said. She'd felt sure that Peter would come this time. Jack said that he'd felt sure Peter would not come.

Peter's absence threatened to become the focus again, but the therapists interrupted, suspecting the "absent member maneuver." The O'Brien's were asked: "Was Peter's absence planned? Were they avoiding other issues by focusing on the family member who was not here?" The family was silent for a moment. When it became clear that no answer would be given, the therapists said the session must continue without talking about Peter.

After a moment Alice began, saying that Jack had criticized her after the last session for not giving the neurological details of his childhood problems. Now, she began to talk about that in great detail. The therapist asked, "Why do you have to do what Jack says?" Alice stated that she had to "serve her family." However, she moved to the present. She expressed great concern about Jack, who had been extremely depressed last Friday night. Jack jumped in angrily to say he was tired of his mother's concern. He immediately began a lengthy discussion of his history teacher's grading practices, and both parents encouraged him to talk about this in great detail. The therapists asked Jack to tell more about his Friday night depression. They felt themselves falling into the family's confusion, but they still attempted to make Jack tell more specifically about what his mother had called "depression." In working with families affected by alcoholism, the therapist must always be alert to mood changes in the alcoholic member, and to any hint of relapse and/or family coverup.

John intervened, saying that Jack had had an "Antabuse reaction," and slowly the story unfolded. Jack, drinking in his room on Friday evening, had developed an Antabuse reaction (a rash, hot flashes, and difficulty breathing). John said he had been concerned about his son, so he had driven him to work that night. However, the family had not even considered calling a doctor, ignoring the potentially serious medical effects of an Antabuse reaction.

The therapist showed concern about the incident, stressing how the three of them intellectualized tremendously about everything, dwelling on academic matters while ignoring serious here-and-now problems. Alice changed the subject and tried to talk about having to satisfy everybody. John said the family was slipping into a situation where the children ruled the parents. He expressed hopelessness about any possibility of change and intense feelings of resentment toward Peter. Jack, becoming annoyed, tried to talk again about his history teacher. Alice began talking about Peter. The session grew chaotic and, in fact, the confusion was even worse than in the first session. What therapeutic strategy could have succeeded then? Could such a chaotic, denying family be given any positive task? The therapists felt almost lost and at this point in the session expressed their confusion and asked the family to deal with one issue at a time. Starting with the father, they asked John to share what was happening to him. Accusations began again and once again an intense argument was raging. Everybody was talking at once; the only people listening were the therapists. An attempt was made to end the session with an emphasis on the seriousness of Jack's Antabuse reaction and their concern about Jack's relapse, but the family couldn't listen.

After the session, the therapists met for a conference. Was family treatment the best approach in this case? Or should the goal be to free Jack, at 19, from this environment, and help him in individual therapy to gain independence without drinking? No contract for family treatment had been agreed upon and, furthermore, the agency was not equipped with emergency services. A crisis could undoubtedly have been created to confront this family with the need for a change, but the therapists were far from certain that this was the correct course.

The question was still unresolved a few days later when Jack's therapist received a phone call from Alice, who said that . Jack would be late for his appointment, but was on the way. When he arrived, Jack had a glazed look on his face, his eyes were red, and his breath smelled of beer. As soon as he sat down, he began talking hysterically. Jack was drunk, and the therapist interrupted to tell him so. Jack whispered that he was going to tell the therapist something personal that must not come up in the family sessions: he had been drinking 3-4 beers a day for the last five days. The therapist questioned about the Antabuse; Jack replied that he had been slipping the pills through his fingers every morning.

The session immediately focused on the drinking, the therapist directly confronting Jack with his condition. Basically, he told Jack that he must take upon himself the responsibility for stopping drinking; that drinking was jeopardizing every area of his life.

Jack's reply was to ramble incoherently about his intense fears, unable to focus on any issue, he merely avoided the question of drinking. The therapist told him they could talk more about these other issues at some other time, when Jack was sober. At the moment, however, the concern was for the immediate problems: How was Jack going to get himself home safely? How would he stop drinking and start on Antabuse again? The therapist also pointed out that Jack should discuss his feelings about having family sessions during a family session. If the O'Briens wanted to stop family sessions, this should be a joint decision.

Jack seemed helpless and confused, but he showed considerable trust. He accepted the therapist's suggestion that he go straight home and rest. The therapist encouraged Jack to call him the next day and tell him how he was doing.

How to best handle a situation like this is a debatable issue. Some therapists would insist on seeing the family together while the patient was intoxicated. Others would work with the alcoholic alone, helping him sober up, and then continue family treatment. Still others would deal immediately with some of the intense feelings brought up by the patient. In Jack's case, the therapists decided on the second strategy, and it was suggested that Mr. and Mrs. O'Brien come for a few couple sessions while Jack was recuperating from his relapse. They agreed to come at the time originally scheduled for family sessions.

But the session proved to be a repetition of the family sessions. Each spouse reported the history of his/her life. In quiet, factual style, both related episodes and symptoms which indicated significant pathology. But they touched on their relationship only in complaining to the therapist about each other.

Was this family ready for changes? Or was only the pathology of each member keeping them all together? If changes were brought about, could the family members collapse?

During this period, Peter arrived unannounced one morning asking to see Jack's therapist. Surprised, but curious to know what had brought him, the therapist saw him. In spite of Jack's descriptions of their infantile bickering, Peter proved to be a tall, quite bright 15-year-old. He conducted himself in an effeminate and artifically adult manner. As he shook the therapist's hand he announced that he was "reporting" on behalf of his brother and would be glad to tell anything that could be helpful. He denied having any problems of his own. Rather romantically he spoke about the fine oak paneling of his family home and his fondness for antiques. He mentioned briefly his love for the theater and his plans to study acting. Finally, he announced that he had no intention of coming for treatment sessions, at which point the therapist merely thanked him for coming in.

We never learned why Peter decided to show up. Perhaps he sensed harbingers of change in the family. Were there changes the therapists were unaware of?

Each member of the O'Brien family exhibited serious problems, and the family structure was pathogenic. Jack's way of being part of the family was to drink. Yet each member seemed to be functioning well in the extrafamilial world. The father held a professional job and was accepted in his field. So too, was the mother at her work. Peter had his life mapped out. Jack had established a good relationship with the individual therapist and was ready to continue treatment.

Exploratory family sessions had clarified some aspects of family structure, and therapeutic possibilities could have been mapped out. But the only way to create real change in this family would have been to push them into crisis. There was a definite possibility that the result would be four people institutionalized, perhaps for life.

An alternative plan was decided upon. Jack would continue his efforts to keep himself from drinking, and individual sessions would determine what changes could be accomplished in other areas of his life. He would soon have to move out of the family, which would free him from having to act out all the family problems.

In conclusion, the O'Briens are an example of a family for which family therapy was not appropriate. In the end, it was decided that since the family was functioning after a fashion and family members were doing well in the outside world, it was best not to try to force change at that time. In a sense, we decided to let the O'Briens continue functioning crazily at home, but well in the outside world. Sometimes therapists must make this decision. Since Jack was willing to continue in individual therapy, we would leave well enough alone with the rest of the family.

The Giacomellis

When a woman does not work outside the home alcoholism can often be hidden for years, with the collusion of the family. In such cases, the family becomes as much a part of the denial as the alcoholic member herself. Uncovering and confronting the alcoholism as an issue may require a massive family intervention, and this, in turn, may create a serious crisis.

The Giacomellis entered treatment when Mr. Giacomelli called a mental health center to request help for his wife who was suffering from nearly-immobilizing depression. At the time, the center was experimenting with a new procedure whereby families were required to come with patients to the initial interview. Arrangements were made to see the Giacomelli family as a unit. Present in the session were Tony, 39; Anina, 38; Carmela, 16; Jack, 14; Don, 12, and Julian, 6.

The central focus was Anina's depression. Everyone agreed that she was the problem. She couldn't keep up with the housework, and every afternoon when the children came home from school they found her lying on the couch suffering from one of her severe headaches. She could no longer participate in most family and community activities, to the point that it had become a severe problem to the family. They all wanted to see a change. Father and the three older children continued talking in terms of "depression," but Julian, reluctantly but determinedly, called the therapist's attention to himself.

"I can tell you what's been happening since I was born," he told her. "For anything before that, you'll have to ask the others." The therapist encouraged Julian to talk. "There's always a glass next to her," Julian said. "And sometimes she doesn't walk straight."

Now that the cat was out of the bag, everyone felt free to talk about Anina's drinking. The whole family knew that she wasn't suffering from headaches; she was intoxicated every afternoon. Episode after episode about her erratic behavior at home was recounted; everyone had an anecdote to contribute. The family kept the mood light. Sometimes even Anina laughed. But to find out that the whole family knew she drank was a severe shock for her.

The session focused on family members' experiences with Anina's drinking, and how deeply it had affected everyone. They felt isolated from extended family and friends. Carmela complained that she never felt free to go out with her friends. She had to come straight home from school to tidy the house and start dinner. Weekends, she left the house only when she knew her father would be home. Jack said he, too, tried to get home from school right away, and he complained about Don, who stayed out till supper time, ate and immediately went out again. Tony explained that his work required long hours, but in the evening he helped Carmela finish the chores. Julian, the baby, was always playing one parent against the other and was growing quite spoiled as a result.

The family members began to complain about each other, each feeling that the other could do more. They all made it plain that it was Anina's role they were trying to fill, but none of them confronted her directly. It was obvious that Anina would have to deal with her drinking problem by herself. The therapist made an appointment with Anina and Tony for the next day. They agreed that it would be important to get a good history of Anina's drinking before formulating any plans for treatment. The first step was already taken: identification of alcoholism as Anina's and the family's problem. Subsequently would come the task of removing it from its central position as the family's curse. It was agreed that family sessions would also be scheduled.

Because Anina reacted positively during the session and made a commitment to work out her problem, the Giacomellis felt sure she could control the situation until the next day. But that evening Anina smuggled a fifth of whiskey into the bathroom, drank most of it, and tried to cut her wrists. She had to be rushed to the emergency room, and from there she was admitted to a detoxification unit.

The therapist visited Anina at the detoxification unit. Anina was angry, resentful and remorseful. Although she had been hospitalized before for various symptoms, she had never before been in such a condition as to be admitted acutely intoxicated. She hated being "in with all these drunks," and she blamed the therapist for revealing a secret she insisted no one had known about until now. Upon the therapist's second visit, Anina, detoxified and clearheaded, was able to see things more realistically, and she greeted the therapist in a friendly way.

Anina was extremely surprised at this second visit—she was amazed that the therapist had considered her worth one subway ride, let alone two. "Why are you so nice to me?" she asked. As with so many alcoholics, she didn't seem to feel she was worth the time of a busy professional. The therapist answered simply that she was concerned about Anina and wanted to see her when she was not under the influence of alcohol.

Feeling accepted, Anina suddenly began to unwind and open up. She talked about her drinking history, the shame of being an alcoholic in a family of "good" people, the years of fear and concealment and ever increasing dependence. She had started to drink shortly after Julian's birth because she was feeling "more and more nervous"—isolated and unable to cope with a household of four active children. A doctor she consulted prescribed tranquilizers, and she took them too. But more and more often, she had found that drinking calmed her down. Now she felt trapped. Her husband was having an affair; he didn't love her any more and who could blame him? The children were all unhappy, and it was her fault. No one could help—all the doctors ever did was write another prescription. At that point, she got out of bed and went to her suitcase, where she'd hidden her pocketbook. She opened it, and it contained enough prescription bottles to stock a medicine chest.

The therapist held out her hand. Anina understood and handed her the pocketbook. "Keep these for me?" she pleaded.

The therapist said she would and began to discuss future plans with Anina, who was to be discharged the next day. Therapy must begin immediately. There would be sessions with the entire family, and with Anina and Tony alone, but the priority was to work on Anina's drinking problem. Anina hesitated, mentioning "depression" and "possible change of life symptoms," but the therapist was firm: the focus must be on alcoholism; that was the central problem. Anina finally agreed.

In some cases it is the patient's own determination to do something about the alcoholism problem that finally facilitates successful treatment. But many times therapy can be initiated by a therapist who shows care and respect for the person's worth, while insisting that the problem be dealt with. In Anina's case, too, her suicide attempt exerted a positive influence. Anina became deeply troubled by the fact that she had been so threatened by the prospect of life without drinking that she tried to cut her wrists. With the therapist's encouragement, she determined to try to find a way out of this trap.

The session the next day included the entire family. The focus was future plans. It was agreed the main target would be Anina's drinking, and that she would take care of that. But the rest of the family would also begin to look at possible changes indicated by the issues brought up in the first session. The family accepted the therapist's advice to treat Anina like any patient recuperating after a period of hospitalization. As Anina regained strength, family sessions would help her resume her tasks and change her position in the family organization.

Anina was referred to A.A., but she never felt comfortable with that group. She was much more comfortable with a therapy group of women alcoholics run by the same therapist. This eventually became a strong network of support, not only for her drinking problem, but also for building her self-esteem.

As Anina began to gain strength through individual and group sessions, the therapist scheduled couple sessions. In one session, she encouraged Anina to discuss her resentment of Tony. Anina knew perfectly well that he had been experimenting with extra-marital relationships, but this had never been mentioned between them. Now she took the opportunity, and Tony began to tell his side. As soon as the area was opened, Anina began to understand how much her drinking, which had made her unavailable as a wife, had contributed to his search for extra-marital warmth and companionship. Winning her husband back began to seem a direct reward for changing, and she set to work with renewed determination.

Tasks designed to encourage the development of support and intimacy within the spouse unit were assigned, and both Anina and Tony moved quickly to find almost forgotten gratifications within that relationship.

One of Anina's main problems was her sense of failure as a mother and housewife. In her patriarchal Italian neighborhood, living in the midst of a house-proud, upwardly mobile working class family, she had felt her lack of contribution keenly. Tasks were assigned to return her to the role she saw as hers. First she was instructed to eat with the family—something she had almost stopped doing during the drinking years. Soon she began to take on the responsibility for cooking and cleaning. Carmela was to help her, but Anina was in charge. Gaining more and more confidence, Anina began to take over once more, freeing Carmela and the other children to go out with their friends, and lead a more normal teenage life. Julian, no longer able to play one parent against the other, also began to grow out of his infantile stance and develop into an outgoing, tough, grade schooler.

As Tony and Anina pulled closer together, they also began to establish better functioning as parents. Together, they set rules, and together, they enforced them. They were concerned about their children; the picture presented in the first session seemed to be confirmed by their descriptions. Carmela was a little mother, Jack was the good older son, Don was an outsider, rebelling and acting out, and Julian was Anina's baby. It was a pattern often seen in alcoholic families.

With the therapist's help, Tony and Anina began to practice acting as a unified parental team in the sessions. Homework assignments continued their practice during the week. This helped them use their new strength as a couple to firm the family foundation.

Unfortunately, Anina's rapid return to competence had forced Carmela into a shatteringly quick role shift. The boys, close to a competent father, had never been quite so badly affected by Anina's disability, but Carmela had taken over as mother and housekeeper in a family with no other girls. Therapist and parents discussed ways of helping her shed responsibility and find compensation in extended family and peer group, but before much could be done, Carmela became pregnant.

Though they were both still in high school, Carmela was adamant: she and her boyfriend must get married. They did, and both dropped out of school. Unable to envision herself in any other role in life, Carmela had engineered a rapid movement into the position of mother of a family of her own.

Tony and Anina both felt Carmela was too young to marry. Several sessions were held to help the family discuss the matter, and finally they agreed to the marriage. Therapy had helped them build up the strength to cope together with this family crisis. But the Giacomellis felt so disgraced that they decided to move to another city. Therapy had to be terminated when they moved, about six months after initiation.

Anina's improvement in therapy had been dramatic. It showed even in her physical appearance, as she began to take care of herself again. For Tony, Anina, and probably the boys, the results were excellent. For Carmela, her mother's improvement had been too rapid.

If therapy had continued, the mother-daughter subsystem would have become a focus. It would have been important to help Anina reach out to her daughter, to help her feel like a daughter again, instead of the mother and housekeeper of the family. Unfortunately, the speed at which Anina resumed her roles pushed Carmela out of the family, toward a family of her own. One could only hope that in the future, circumstances would open her life to the opportunities her mother's drinking had closed off during her adolescence.

The Richardsons

Alcoholism in a parent can have a devastating effect on a child, who may entirely lack the security of knowing that his needs will be provided for. If such a child comes to the attention of a therapist, he may be misread, leading to a situation in which therapy focuses on presumed faults within the child instead of the lack of stability in his most vital context.

When Peter Richardson was ten, his school referred him to the pediatric department of a nearby hospital. Peter's teachers complained that he was hyperactive, unable to concentrate or keep still. He also presented severe reading problems. With these symptoms, the obvious course was to have Peter be evaluated by a child psychiatrist, who made a diagnosis of early schizophrenia. Peter began individual therapy and remedial reading classes.

That hospital was organized in the traditional way whereby a psychiatrist worked with a child, and a social worker had to see the family in auxiliary therapy. An appointment was made with Peter's mother, Collette.

The first meeting was scheduled for 11 a.m. As the social worker shook hands with Collette, she smelled liquor on her breath. Without embarrassment and with a very comfortable attitude, she asked Collette if she had been drinking before coming to the session. Collette, surprised by the social worker's directness, admitted with some embarrassment that she'd had to have a drink before coming.

The story of the Richardsons began to unfold. Collette had been drinking heavily since her late teens, and presently, she was unable to control her alcohol intake. As she spoke about herself, she also revealed that her husband Sean was an active alcoholic. The session shifted from a focus on Peter "the schizophrenic" to a concentration on drinking problems.

The social worker decided to work with both parents in cooperation with the alcoholism division of the hospital. The first step was to see if both Collette and Sean were willing to look into the problem. Both agreed, and furthermore, Sean agreed to be hospitalized for detoxification. Collette, with the therapist's support, was able to stop drinking without medical intervention. Both were referred to A.A., though Sean became more involved than Collette.

As the parents' functioning improved, they began to look into the organization of the family. Peter, too, was showing improvements, and the therapist, greatly encouraged, arranged for the Richardsons to be seen as a family. Sean had been sober during this period, though he was still unemployed and in poor health. Collette had recovered enough to hold a job, but she could only remain sober for a few weeks at a time, then relapse.

As soon as information on the Richardson family became available to the family therapy team, it became obvious that Peter, diagnosed as an early schizophrenic by an individual therapist because of wildly erratic behavior, was actually a barometer of his parents' functioning. Peter was Collette's son by her first marriage; he had never known his own father. Collette had married Sean in a drunken stage when Peter was two. All his life the child had lived with two active, heavy drinkers. Drunkenness was the normal lifestyle of this family; Peter didn't know people could live any other way. Without friends, he spent his time in the apartment watching TV, with the dog for company. Often he was the one who called the local liquor store for a delivery. When his mother was functioning well, Peter would begin to do better in school, keep his appointments with the psychiatrist, and attend his remedial reading classes. As soon as his mother started drinking again, his functioning would become "schizophrenic."

When family therapy began, Sean was the outsider in the family. He had been sober for six months, but he kept himself busy with A.A. activities from early evening until late at night, then slept till noon, unable to mobilize himself for any other activity. Collette was working, but she had become a chain smoker and was now in a stage of denial about her drinking. As she saw it, she occasionally took a drink or two. She thought she could control her drinking and remain a social drinker, an idea not borne out by her past history.

Both parents came from wealthy families. Sean had a Ph.D., with honors, from a prestigious university, but he had never been able to practice his profession. Collette had been exclusively educated and had once tried a career as a dancer. They had both run through their inheritances, and the family was now on welfare plus whatever Collette earned as a temporary secretary during her periods of sobriety.

The family history showed that Collette had the capacity to quit drinking, without medication or hospitalization. But she would always start again. Sean, though now sober for six months, was immobilized by the long years of drinking. He showed no self-esteem, and no capacity to feel or express emotion. Nevertheless, both parents saw Peter as the sick member of the family. They came to family therapy only in an effort to help their son. Very discouraged by the diagnosis of early schizophrenia, they were afraid that nothing could be done for Peter.

By the second family session it was time to arrange summer camp for Peter. He was afraid to leave home, terrified that his mother would die while he was away. Because it was necessary to pull the therapeutic team together, a session with Peter's psychiatrist, the social worker, the remedial reading teacher and the family therapists was arranged.

Peter was unusually restless during the session, lying on the floor most of the time and repeatedly recounting the experience of a child he had heard of who went to camp and who had received a letter saying his mother had died. Neither his parents nor the therapists were able to calm Peter down, or even get him to sit in a chair.

How could Peter be reassured? We suggested that Collette keep in touch with him, and she promised to send him a postcard at camp every day.

The therapists were all concerned about the outcome, knowing that Collette was still drinking off and on. It was a difficult session, too, for Peter's psychiatrist, who was psychoanalytically oriented. It turned out that sharing their experience with a group of professionals was reassuring to these parents. It was decided that Sean and Collette would continue therapy as a couple while Peter was away. The plan proceeded further, Peter did go to camp, and Collette kept her promise to write him daily.

Unfortunately, the Richardsons still insisted on believing that Peter was the sick family member. They could not progress further to the point of dealing with the problems in their own relationship, and Sean could not be brought to focus on his relationship with his stepson. It was amazing how available they were to treatment, but how difficult it was for them to see that any change in themselves was necessary. It seemed that they would come to sessions willingly and indefinitely, as long as the subject was only Peter's condition.

When Peter returned from camp the Richardsons were referred to a multi-family group then being formed. A multi-family group is a "hybrid" of family therapy and group therapy, according to Laqueur. Like family therapy, its target is the dysfunctioning family system, but it is a method that allows feedback from a "suprasystem"—the outside world, as represented by other families. In multi-family therapy, roles in the single family tend to diffuse through cross-family interaction. Problem members are different in every family, so that a child with a drinking father, for instance, can relate in the multi-family group to a better-functioning father from another family. In addition, observation of how other families function can provide modeling for members of the group.

The goals of multi-family therapy are:

1. To decrease denial via sharing and identification.
2. Help "well" family members identify themselves as part of the homeostatic functioning of the family.
3. To develop problem solving skills through the use of other group members as sounding boards and modelers of different skills.

In the group the Richardson family agreed to join, two of the families had children Peter's age. There was alcoholic parental dysfunctioning in some of the other families, but the Johnson family had a strong father who saw himself as his own sons' chief disciplinarian. Along with his authority, he had the capacity to guide, and to communicate warmth. The therapists hoped that Mr. Johnson could become Peter's surrogate father, and influence his behavior. It was also possible that the group would be able to break through Collette's denial of her alcoholism, confronting her from the perspective of people in the same boat.

The multi-family group gave Peter siblings, and the figure of a strong father, who could also be a model for Sean. When Peter became restless, Mr. Johnson could help him set controls. The Johnson boys, both bright, healthy children, discussed life situations with Peter and helped him face them in a more realistic way. In one session, for example, the children began to discuss sex. Peter had been sexually used by some men in the local park. He told of his experiences, expressing his confusion and hurt. The Johnson family helped him talk about it, and Peter was able to work through the problem with the help of the adults and children in the group.

For the first time, we felt that Peter was moving toward genuine improvement. He was relating to people, speaking when spoken to, and beginning to be more relaxed. The multi-family group gave him a family context which showed him care and understanding.

Unfortunately, Sean's passive approach to life continued, and Collette still had ups and downs with her drinking. Furthermore, the family had lost its identified patient, and the Richardsons started to feel the pressure to look at what they were doing themselves. Without warning, Collette had a bad relapse, and this time Sean started to drink again. Soon the situation was entirely out of control, with both parents intoxicated and unreachable, and Peter staying home from school and sessions in order to help keep the household together. The old style of life returned. The therapists, the Johnson family, and Sean's A.A. sponsor all tried to reach the family to persuade the parents to take steps toward detoxification, with no success.

The professional team decided on a home visit. Peter let the therapist in. The apartment was a shambles. Both parents were intoxicated, semi-clothed, Sean lying on the bed and Collette on the couch. The team had to make a decision. They agreed that Peter must be removed from the house, for his own protection and in the hope of creating therapeutic crisis for this family. Peter left with the therapist.

As soon as Peter was gone, Collette admitted herself for detoxification. Sean called his A.A. fellows. They came over, helped him clean the apartment, then took him to the hospital's detoxification unit. As the therapists had hoped, the crisis mobilized the Richardsons to stop drinking. But Collette resented the fact that her son had been removed while she lay intoxicated. Two days later she picked Peter up at the shelter on her way home from the detoxification unit. She refused to have any further contact with the therapeutic team.

How can this case be evaluated? For Peter, the results were good—we know this because he continued with remedial reading classes, and we were able to follow his progress with his teacher. In the combination of individual, family, and family group treatment, Peter had learned that life can be different—that families can be organized around something other than drinking and fighting. His remedial reading teacher felt he was integrating this experience into his life, and his continuing good relationship with her was another positive experience for this child.

The prognosis for Peter's parents was more guarded. Sean had become actively involved in A.A. and had had some success in maintaining sobriety. He might soon be ready to focus on himself, though it seemed it would be some time before he had the strength to pick up the roles of husband, father, and provider. For Collette the prognosis was poorest. Though she now saw her drinking as a problem in the family, she had never accepted the fact that she must deal with it by stopping her alcohol intake. I met her some six years later at a different agency, still unenthusiastically "seeking help" for her "drinking problem."

The Harrisons

Exchanges within the alcoholic family develop "around" the skew caused by the alcoholic member's incapacity. Even if the latter attains sobriety, the patterns established over the drinking years may continue to hamper individual and family development, unless family members become aware of the need for change.

Fred and Clara Harrison came to therapy after hearing me deliver a talk at a combined A.A. and Al-Anon meeting about "communication in the family." Fred, 44, was an alcoholic who had succeeded in maintaining sobriety for five years with the help of A.A. He held a responsible job at an export firm and was very involved with the A.A. program. Clara worked as an executive secretary, was attending night school, and was equally involved with Al-Anon. When she called for an appointment, she expressed dissatisfaction with her life. She couldn't elaborate much further besides indicating that my talk had made her aware that there was a "lack of communication" in her family, and between Fred and her.

A meeting with the couple was arranged. After the usual social chitchat, I asked the Harrisons to describe their relationship. Clara immediately began to complain about the lack of contact between herself and Fred, then continued with a description of the family at present. Clara saw herself as being away from home most of the time, busy with work, school, and Al-Anon. She spent her lunch hours in a bookstore; at home, she read. Mary, 20, did most of the housework, took care of the family, and was taking some college courses part-time. Rosalie, 21, was just back from a long vacation in Europe. Freddie, 19, had dropped out of college and was in the process of looking for a job. He was very disoriented about his future.

Clara paused and Fred began to talk about himself. He was busy working and very much involved with A.A., where he was sponsoring several young men. At home he took care of some of the household chores. His particular job was to go shopping with Mary on Saturday morning, so Clara could sleep late.

This brought the couple back to Clara's initial statement that the two of them did very little together. It seemed that during the drinking years, the Harrison family had developed the not uncommon pattern of allowing the children to take on the tasks of the drinking parent as well as of the overburdened nondrinking parent. This pattern, persisting for years, had seemed normal to the Harrisons. But now several things were happening and Clara, at 43, was facing significant changes in her life. They were negotiating the purchase of a new house, which would mean a move away from Clara's mother, who lived next door. At the same time, the children were developing plans for leaving home. Thus, circumstances would soon force Clara to be mainly a wife, instead of a daughter and mother. Did her complaint of "lack of communication" indicate that she had been thinking a lot about herself? What would be left for her when they moved away from her mother and the children were gone?

Why the Harrisons were coming to therapy was slowly being uncovered. They were facing one of the normal crises of any family development: the "empty nest syndrome." But as always happens with alcoholic families, their problem was exacerbated by abnormal patterns developed over the years of alcoholic disruptive behavior. Ideally, the forties and fifties are a time for adults to use their freedom to embark on new personal possibilities and enrich the spouse subsystem which is once again the basic family unit. Here, Fred's drinking had put an immense distance between this couple. He had turned to A.A, and during the years of his recovery, Clara had become strongly involved with Al-Anon. As many Al-Anon members do, she had interpreted "independence" as overinvolvement with extrafamilial activities. So although she had learned to focus her psychic energy on constructive activity for herself, her role in the family was still largely what it had been during Fred's drinking years. Protected by the children and their premature assumption of parental roles, she had become the outsider. But now, middle-aged, with her children leaving home, and not functioning fully as mother and spouse, Clara felt fundamentally threatened.

She spoke of feeling incompetent as a woman, wife, and mother. She wondered if Fred was sexually attracted to the young men he was sponsoring in A.A. Doubts about her own sexuality made her have doubts about Fred's. That took Fred entirely by surprise and his response was reassurance, with a great deal of tenderness. The exchange continued, and Clara shared with him a little more about her feelings, and the need to reassess their relationship as husband and wife.

Slowly it was dawning on Clara that she was feeling incompetent as a woman and, as such, was unable to share a fulfilled sexual life with her husband. She began to talk about her image of herself, the problems of separating from her mother and children. The resentments of the drinking years still smoldered, but there was also an inkling of warmth in the relationship which gave hope for rebuilding the marriage.

The main goal of therapy at this point was to help the couple open up to each other, start trusting, and work on developing the intimacy both wanted. Sessions were scheduled for this purpose, and many changes were accomplished as they both concentrated on learning to trust each other again. The therapist assigned several tasks. They were to meet for lunch several times a week and plan weekend trips away from the children. If they were going out to A.A. or Al-Anon meetings in the evenings, they were to leave the house together and return together. In therapy sessions, they were encouraged to express their needs and discuss what they wanted from each other. They were really surprised at how much they learned about each other in a short time.

When this was well underway, I suggested incorporating the children in the ongoing therapy. Fred and Clara understood the importance of this step and agreed to have them in a session. However, since everybody in the family had a busy schedule, the therapist had to arrange to meet them on a Saturday morning.

Rosalie, Mary and Freddie were good-looking young people, casually but carefully dressed. They showed some anxiety, but were able to relax as the session started.

The therapist began by soliciting a picture of the family as they saw it. Mary picked up immediately, starting to describe a family with an actively drinking father. She said that Fred didn't participate in family life and, as a result, she, her sister and brother felt sorry for their mother and had to help and protect her.

The therapist pointed out that perhaps Mary was describing the family during Fred's drinking years and asked Mary if this was the situation in the present. How did she see the family today? Mary immediately began to complain that her family exploited her. Over the years she had taken on the housework. She was a neat and orderly person and worked hard to keep the house clean, while the others neither appreciated nor respected her.

As soon as Mary stopped, Freddie picked up and started to complain about Mary. He said Mary continued to treat him like a child. For instance, when he left for a date, she would come to the door to inspect his dress, and he hated it.

Rosalie sat back just listening to Mary and Freddie complain. She had been able to escape and develop her life outside of the family, leaving Mary and Freddie to their overinvolved roles. Now just back from a trip to Europe, she was hunting for her own apartment, while struggling to keep her two jobs.

After five years of sobriety, the children in this family were still functioning in the patterns developed during the drinking years. Mary was the substitute mother, and although she resented the role she had played all these years and felt hurt that no one appreciated her efforts, she had not yet relinquished her place. Freddie was still treated as the baby.

The therapist suggested that Clara discuss with Mary her budding desire, expressed during a couple sessions, to take on more of a role within the family. Clara, still intimidated by her daughter, shook her head silently.

Fred had been sitting in the background, seemingly an outsider. Still on the task of eliciting the family's picture of themselves in the present, the therapist asked Freddie how he was getting along with his father. Freddie replied briefly that there were no problems, but was interrupted by Clara's reminding him of what had happened during the years when Fred was drinking. At that time, Fred would promise his son they would go out on the boat on Saturday morning. They would get to the marina, Fred would go into the bar, and they would never cast off. "I didn't care," Freddie said. "After a while I got my own boat."

Was Clara using Freddie in this instance to express some of her own lingering resentments? Or was she assuming an old role?

Fred had sobered when Freddie was 13-14, but he had made little attempt to get closer to his children, particularly his son. Now in the session he gave it a try, saying he knew Freddie was having a difficult time trying to find a job. Fred indicated he would like to help, but Freddie rejected him immediately. There was a painful silence.

Suddenly, Clara broke the impasse by putting herself on the hot seat, thus protecting both Fred and Freddie. Facing Mary, she said that she planned to take over the role of the woman of the house. Surprised, Mary challenged that, emphasizing her mother's lack of time due to overinvolvement with outside activities. Clara retorted that she and Fred had already discussed this, and she had decided to give up something, most probably her evening classes. This was significant in so far as it showed that Clara had built up enough trust in Fred to use him as a support in front of the children. Mary could not immediately accept her mother's change—which would mandate a change in her own acquired pattern—and challenged again. Clara asked to be given a chance, and Fred nodded approval.

The family began to discuss practical matters, and everyone agreed to cooperate. Clara pointed out that her taking on more of the chores would give Mary the option of returning to school full-time—something Mary had been talking about for the past year. Mary looked up in surprise and an expression of happiness crossed her face.

Since only one session would be held with this entire family, the therapist was forced to make some interpretations about the family organization. She questioned Rosalie, Mary and Freddie, wondering if they were still walking on eggs, protecting Fred, afraid that he might go back to his drinking. The three of them agreed. Fred picked this up immediately and told the children this was his problem, and he was taking care of it, as he had for the past five years.

The therapist stated that the adopted protective patterns in the family remaining through misunderstanding were no longer appropriate and must be broken. Both parents and children had to recognize that the situation had changed and act accordingly.

Freddie was in trouble. He resented his father, but was not able to deal with him. The issues of father and son, barely touched on in this family, would require much work.

Mary must find something outside her family to fill her own time and needs, instead of continuing as substitute mother. Rosalie was doing well, though there were some indications that she was following her mother's pattern by overfilling her days.

These interpretations were made because the therapist sensed both strength and readiness for change in this family. In spite of the problems originally caused by alcoholism and now persisting in its wake, there was a lot of health inherent in this family (a tribute to both Fred and Clara), which could be used to mobilize the family for change.

Couple sessions continued, focusing on developing intimacy. As the Harrisons became stronger and closer, they reported that Mary was much less involved with them. She did begin full-time school, and gradually freed herself from household responsibilities. When the family moved to their new house, Mary got her own apartment.

Fred continued trying to reach his son. One day he called the therapist requesting to come for a session with his son. He said that Freddie was very upset because he still couldn't find a job, but at the same time he wouldn't accept his father's help. It appeared that father and son couldn't talk to each other. This move by Fred to delineate a new subsystem in the family was an interesting additional proof that the Harrisons were continuing to seek change.

I arranged an early appointment. When they came to the session, Fred said immediately that they had been able to start talking and to share some ideas. The mere fact that he made the decision to call the therapist for help in communicating with Freddie strengthened his ability to open up the dialogue between them.

In the session Fred explained to Freddie that although he did not want to impose his own values, he did want Freddie to know that he respected him as a young adult and wanted to do whatever he could to make things easier for him while he was looking for work. This, in turn, helped Freddie to ease up and he managed to respond that although he had never felt close to his father, he understood that Fred was trying to help. He was willing to work on a relationship as long as his father understood that he had to do things his own way. He proceeded to expound on his plans. Fred pointed out ways he could help. It was agreed they would work on handling things this way in the future and call the therapist if they ran into problems.

The Harrisons' case is a good example of two basic therapeutic principles. First, it is often advisable to bring about changes in the family by first attempting to rebuild the spouses' relationship. Assuming the couple is willing and ready, they can be helped in pulling together into a team. When work with the children begins, a foundation for change has already been established. Second, family members of any age may have to learn that complementarity does not conflict with autonomy. For Clara, autonomy had meant being an outsider. She had to learn that she could relate to Fred as a wife without sacrificing her sense of self. Freddie, at a very difficult age, had to learn that living his own life did not preclude his need to develop a relationship with a father he had never really known.

In spite of Fred's sustained sobriety, the Harrison family had remained trapped in their old patterns, with both Fred and Clara working on their individual development without integrating their changes into a family structure. As a result, a stalemate developed over the years that was hampering the children's growth and undercutting a source of support for both spouses. Once the barriers erected by all members of the family started to be removed in therapy, they began to create the missing links and build up the existing ones.

The Clatworthys

"Ghetto Alcoholism" is often more than alcoholism. It is all the problems of alcoholism, combined with the stresses of poverty and/or discrimination. A low income family does not have the safety margin that often helps better-off families cope with alcoholism. There are no seminars on alcoholism and the executive, no company health insurance plan. Friends and relatives may lack the resources to help as they would like. Furthermore, to a striving, lower middle class black family like the Clatworthys, to whom moving up was almost a religion, alcoholism can carry a double stigma. Not only is it a personal "weakness," it is also a threat to the children's future.

The Clatworthys were referred to me by a job supervisor, who said that Mrs. Clatworthy, 35, was potentially one of his best workers. But over the past year and a half she had been failing in job performance. He had suggested that she call a doctor, but she had explained that the problem was not her health, but her worry over her two sons. They were playing hooky and no longer working up to capacity in school. She had taken Daniel, 16, to a child guidance clinic at the school's suggestion, but nothing had happened and she was very discouraged. She didn't know what else to do.

The job supervisor told me that the Clatworthys were an upwardly mobile black family, highly invested in escaping from the cycle of limited education and limited opportunity. Jean, who worked as a file clerk, was determined to see all her children through school and to live what she called "a decent life." This was an uphill struggle, the supervisor said, and the family had had to move to cheaper apartments several times. But the drive remained. The supervisor expressed concern because Mrs. Clatworthy's job was the only chance she and her children had to break the poverty cycle.

The supervisor mentioned one more thing—something he said he doubted even the children knew. Mr. Clatworthy had been an alcoholic. After many years of increasing alcohol abuse, he had developed cirrhosis of the liver. One day he collapsed and died in the street. Within days Jean had moved, with Daniel, then 9, Steven, 8, and Linette, 4. Mandy was born four months later. The move took the family away from the support of a concerned extended family and community network. But Jean Clatworthy had to get far away from anyone who knew her shame: an alcoholic husband and father.

The supervisor suggested that Jean bring the children to me with the purpose of making an assessment of the family. Jean agreed, and an appointment was made.

After a few cancelled appointments Jean appeared with her four children. The children were well-groomed, but cautious and reserved. When they entered the room they sat in a circle. Jean looked shy and withdrawn, as contrasted to the children's cautious appraisal of the therapist. She chose a seat outside the circle. Invited to join the group, she did so, but without changing expression.

Jean started to list the family problems. She focused immediately on her difficulties dealing with her two sons, particularly Daniel, now 16. Lately he had become more disobedient and defiant. He insisted on going back to the old neighborhood on weekends in spite of her disapproval. Jean added that she had been a widow for six years, and found it difficult to manage the children, the household chores and a job.

Daniel reacted angrily. He said he couldn't understand why they had to come to "this place" to discuss "family affairs" they could take care of at home. But Jean reemphasized her need to get help. She felt progressively more and more unable to do everything alone. She recognized that the children were trying to help her, especially the girls and Steven, whom she described as a good boy. But that was not enough.

The therapist picked up on Daniel's anger at being at the agency, and asked Jean if she had explained to the children why they were coming here. Jean said that she'd "just told them that they had to come." This gave the therapist an opportunity to involve the children in the therapeutic process by questioning each of them. Were they aware of the problems their mother had just mentioned? She met with silence. No one volunteered information, so the therapist tried to draw out each child in turn, going around the circle. Sensing the children's wariness, she proceeded gently, working her way cautiously around.

Steven ignored the question and barely indicated that he'd heard. Linette echoed her mother: the family problems were the boys' disobedience and fighting. When Daniel's turn came he pinpointed himself as the problem, the troublemaker, and again he expressed annoyance at being there. He repeated that he couldn't see any reason for coming. When I spoke to Mandy she smiled, looking at her mother and sister. Daniel immediately interrupted, saying "She doesn't know; leave her alone!" At this point Steven also spoke like his mother, focusing on the fighting, but said there was no real problem.

The family members were very tense, controlling their emotions. Steven was sitting very quiet and rigid, holding on to his hat and staring at the floor. Daniel was still defiant and protective of the others. They all appeared confused and unsure of how they should answer. It was hard to tell whether they were defying their mother or protecting her, and there was no way of knowing whether this reflected their behavior at home.

Mrs. Clatworthy insisted again that the main problem was disciplining the children. She couldn't do it alone. "They would have listened to their father," she said, but they wouldn't mind her.

Since the father had been mentioned, the therapist asked about him. There was a silence, then Mrs. Clatworthy said briefly that he'd died quite suddenly before Mandy was born.

Daniel interrupted, saying that the father was the problem. It seemed the "ghost" in the family was surfacing. The therapist tried again to focus on the father's death and again she met with silence. Did they ever speak of him, or mourn his loss? Was he ever mentioned in the family?

A family secret is symptomatic of a family's problems. Jean's life was dominated by the spectre of alcoholism. It was not only a threat in itself, but also a symbol of everything she was trying to escape. As a result, the father's alcoholism was strongly influencing the way she saw her children.

Jean changed the subject abruptly, explaining that the move after her husband's death had taken her children away from her family and their old neighborhood. She couldn't afford the rents in that area, so she'd had to take what she could get. The children had had to change schools, and it was difficult to get back to see her family.

Daniel complained that he was forbidden to spend Sundays with Grandmother, visiting friends in the old neighborhood. His mother thought he was going out to drink and smoke pot. But he was not. He just liked to see his family. Steven added that he liked to visit too. He was very close to one of his uncles, and that was the only chance he had to see him.

It seemed that Jean's mother had taken care of the children even before Mr. Clatworthy's death. The therapist asked herself whether Jean's move had put her in the position of having to learn to be a mother, as well as a single parent. Had the children experienced not only the loss of a father, but also the loss of their primary caretaker?

In order to set some working goals, the therapist asked the family members what they would like to change. Again silence fell; the only one who replied was Linette, who said the furniture was in poor condition and the linoleum needed replacing. This was again corrected by Daniel, who seemed very protective of the image of his family.

By the end of the session the therapist felt that little had been accomplished. The strongest impression was derived from the impact of the father's death in the family function. She thought that mourning for the father would be important for the Clatworthys, especially if Jean and the older children could bring up some of the good things they remembered. By talking about the father, they might also come to understand that he was a sick person and not just a drunkard of whom they must be ashamed. Perhaps Jean could learn to detach from the shame which had been such an influence on her life.

None of this was expressed to the family, but Jean may well have picked up the impression that Mr. Clatworthy would have to be discussed. Although she agreed to come back for a few more sessions, the family never returned.

After several appointments had been broken, rescheduled, and broken again, the therapist reached out, telephoning Jean. Jean said frankly that she felt Mr. Clatworthy's death would have to be discussed in family sessions, and she didn't want that to happen. Daniel, the oldest, remembered his father's drinking, but the others, the girls, "didn't know." She wanted them to have the image of a good father, not a drunkard. Some of her anger against her husband showed for the first time in this conversation, but when the therapist again suggested that they set another appointment, Jean refused firmly. She simply would not take the risk of opening this area for the children and herself.

A therapeutic contract might have been made to continue without talking about the father. But this would have been extremely difficult, and probably Jean could never have trusted the therapist to keep away from this area.

Furthermore, concentrating on Jean's difficulties might have raised the prospect of losing her job, since Jean knew her job supervisor knew me. Focusing on changes would have been difficult if not impossible. Under the circumstances, I accepted Jean's decision.

Jean Clatworthy's life was one long flight from alcoholism. The dreadful secret had impelled her to move away from the extended family which could have been her support. In trying to prove herself the mother she felt society expected her to be, she was failing to recognize the needs of her growing children. Her great fear of drinking, as well as pot, blinded her to their adolescent search for independence. She was trying to keep them home, safe, and her very concern was driving them to escape.

Much could have been done to help the Clatworthys, through Al-Anon, Alateen, alcoholism education, and helping Jean and the boys learn how to negotiate in a manner more appropriate to a mother and her teenage children. But unless some crisis brought Jean back to therapy, her decision would have to stand.

The Collins

Some alcoholism programs have developed longer term (30 to 90 days) inpatient rehabilitation units for those in need of a temporary sheltered environment after detoxification. The populations served by these programs come mostly from the very deteriorated victims of long years of drinking. Some patients, however, have no home to return to, and the halfway house becomes their next step. The main modality of treatment is group therapy, with reinforced life learning experiences. From this background, the individual may start to re-enter community life. Specific programs attempt a further step, namely, a return to the family of origin. The latter approach may create differences of opinion among therapists.

John Collins was admitted to an alcoholism rehabilitation unit at the request of his sisters, Mary and Cathleen. Their information was that John, 65, had been drinking all his life.

He had been hospitalized for alcoholism several times, but never followed treatment recommendations after discharge. More than ever, the sisters were concerned because John, now in very poor health, was facing mandatory retirement. In the intervening years he had isolated himself from the family and had no home to go to. Also, he was becoming more violent during drinking sprees, and if he came to live with them he might become dangerous.

John was admitted to the unit, but before the alcoholism counselor had the first session with the patient, she was bombarded by phone calls from both sisters. They were full of questions and advice and called repeatedly to find out whether John had exploded and perhaps become violent.

The counselor met with John and returned very confused. Prepared by the sisters to take precautions against a possibly violent man, she found herself talking to a submissive, withdrawn individual ready to do anything the counselor suggested.

John offered the following information. He was the oldest of five siblings, and the only one who never married. His father had died when they were all very young, and John left home shortly afterwards. For a while he drifted across the country and finally landed a job as a deckhand on an ore freighter. He had remained with the company ever since, working his way up to first mate. "And I'm the best damn first mate in the service," he growled. The counselor encouraged him to talk about his job, and discovered that John was extremely bitter about the "fool rule" that was going to force him into retirement in a few months. John was adamant; he was going to fight that with everything he had. He'd get the union to back him and force the company to keep him on.

As the meeting unfolded, the counselor began to realize that John actually knew there was no hope he could retain his job. But he simply could not envision any alternative to the life he had led for forty years. He was started on individual therapy, made some progress and began to think more realistically about his future. At that point the counselor suggested having a few sessions with the participation of his sisters. John agreed submissively, and I was called in as a consultant in family therapy. Both sisters were anxious to come, and a meeting was arranged.

As soon as we met Mary, the youngest of the siblings, we recognized a family powerhouse. An officer in the Salvation Army, Mary radiated righteous authority. Her sister Cathleen was small and thin, fragile and doll-like. John greeted them politely, then sat down to stare at the floor.

Mary described John in no uncertain terms as the family lost sheep. He'd been a drinker all his life and squandered his money. Cathleen, with tears in her eyes, expressed a desire only to see her big brother improve and get closer to the family. Ever since their father's death, she had hoped that John, her eldest brother, would take the father's place in the family. But he never had. He had failed them all. Mary agreed that his job was the cause for his lost contact with the family. He'd spent most of his life traveling and when he did come for visits, he stayed in a hotel and spent his vacation drinking. Now he had no place to go.

John sat in the corner like a little boy being scolded by a parent, occasionally looking to Cathleen for support. The therapist tried to draw him out a little and talk about his retirement. John growled that this was unfair. The company was pushing him out after nearly 40 years of hard work. He appreciated his sisters' desire to help, but his problem was forced retirement. He'd always been a traveling man. What was he supposed to do now? Mary interjected that drinking wasn't a solution. At that point silence fell. It was clear that Mary and John put emphasis on different issues.

John was trying to prove that he was not a bum. But Mary repeated that she wanted to help John, but not to go back home to live with them. He must find a place of his own to settle. The message was clear: we want you, but we don't want to take care of you. John found his sisters' behavior very confusing.

Their welcome was forgiving, but conditional. Though he never mentioned an interest in going back to live with them, they made it clear this would not be acceptable.

Easter was approaching, and both sisters were anxious to have John spend it with the family. They talked about nieces and nephews and how much these were looking forward to meeting him again. It was their belief that the holiday spirit would make his visit much easier.

Toward the end of the session the tension had eased. Before they left, Mary took some money from her purse and offered it to John. Asked why she was giving John money, she explained that she collected his paychecks, banked them for him, and gave him cash as he needed it. Suddenly, it became apparent that he had maintained contact with the family. John accepted the money but studied his sister's face to see if he was to be scolded for irresponsibility once again. Both women began to cry. Here was an older brother, they said, unable to function on his own. John didn't try to defend himself. He seemed to be used to these scenes.

In a subsequent session we learned that John had gone to Easter Sunday dinner with the family. But, unknown to the sisters, he had invited another man from the rehabilitation unit to accompany him. John admitted in the session that he didn't feel strong enough to face the family alone. He'd hoped that the presence of a stranger would keep the family from talking about his problems. This session became a repetition of the first, with both women saying again and again how much the family wanted to help John. The counselor pointed out, however, that on the one hand they were treating John as an incompetent man, and on the other, they were urging him to become head of the family. If John was to take charge of his life, their attitude must change. Helped by this interpretation John began to "open up" and share some of his own doubts about the future. However, he did not feel strong enough to make promises about specific changes. In the meantime, he continued in individual and group therapy. His self-esteem was growing. He actively participated in the Rehab Unit's daily activities, in which he proved to himself that he could socialize without drinking.

Since plans for discharge had to be arranged, the counselor decided to present John's case at a staff meeting. Interestingly enough, the discussion here centered around the treatment John should be offered. The question divided the staff. Assuming he would remain sober, should we leave him to continue a free, unattached life on discharge? Or should we try to encourage closeness to his family until he developed his own social network? The conflict was never resolved. At discharge, the counselor arranged for John to go to a halfway house and never learned the outcome. The ideal approach in John's case would have been to use the family and A.A. as basic support. However, family therapy would not have meant returning John to live with his sisters in the role of a father figure. Individual therapy would be added to help him chart an independent pursuit of personal wishes.

The McCarthys

Therapy of an alcoholic family should always include the alcoholic member, and abuse of alcohol should be one of the therapeutic targets. Unfortunately, making such a contract is not always possible. In some cases the alcoholic proves genuinely unreachable. In others, he simply refuses to commit himself to therapy. When this happens, we must still attempt to free the other family members from the effects alcoholism has on their lives. A change in the life of the family members will usually, in some measure, reach the alcoholic.

The McCarthys were living the comfortable life of the western small-town upper middle class when Richard's company transferred them to New York City. Lisa was extremely reluctant to leave her family and childhood friends, but the couple agreed that Lisa would make plans to go back to Nebraska whenever she felt too lonely in New York.

Lisa had been a devoted wife and mother, but also close to her own family. Now the children were grown and out of the home. Richard Jr., 24, and Jim, 22, were married. Mary Ann, 20, was away at college. Richard's job had always required a lot of traveling, which Lisa had never minded as long as she had her own family close by. Now she found herself on her own in a strange city. She seemed to lack the resources to come to terms with these changes in her life, and for the first time she was confronted with a fact that she had not recognized up to now: Richard was a "problem drinker."

Lisa began to lose weight and developed some digestive problems. Very concerned about her health, she consulted a doctor and volunteered some concern about emotional discomforts. She was depressed and very anxious, especially at night. Her husband often came home late, she said, and suddenly found herself talking about her husband. How Richard was prolonging the "happy hour" until 9 or 10 at night. How he often just made it to his easy chair before falling asleep, unable to talk to her, or join her in eating the dinners she carefully kept warm. As the doctor questioned her gently, she found herself confiding how one night she had come home to find Richard unconscious on the floor. She couldn't even get him to come to the phone to talk to the children these days. He was almost always "asleep."

Lisa was lucky. The doctor she had picked knew something about alcoholism, and more important, believed that wives of alcoholics can be helped. So instead of reaching for his prescription pad, he firmly instructed Lisa to get in touch with Al-Anon.

This upset Lisa badly, but she decided to attend a few Al-Anon meetings and find out what this was about. The first meeting frightened her, but she found the factual information very useful. She began to understand the fact that Richard was an alcoholic and to learn how other women were facing similar situations. Lisa decided to continue with Al-Anon. She also made an appointment to see me.

At this point Lisa was underweight and shy, still terrified after eight months in the big city. She traveled only by bus, a recognizable thing from "home," and refused to enter the subway. She presented herself as a highly incompetent woman, lost without the guidance of her family.

She was in great need of support, but the only people in New York she could resort to were her husband's colleagues and their wives. That frightened her because any discussion of her situation would reveal Richard's drinking problem and might jeopardize his job. Unable as yet to trust the Al-Anon group, she pleaded for help, anxious to try anything to feel better.

We agreed that Lisa would start individual therapy. I told her that at some point, it would be necessary to involve Richard. Lisa said he would never agree and preferred to focus on making herself more competent.

The therapist's goal at this point was to help Lisa concentrate on aspects of her life apart from Richard's drinking, build up her strength and capabilities, and develop her own interests and life goals, as was appropriate for any woman her age. In this way, I hoped Lisa could reduce her worry about Richard's drinking and get off his back. An improvement in Lisa could be a way of changing Richard and possibly reaching out to get him to explore the possibility of therapy.

Lisa began to improve rapidly as her strength and competence developed under therapy. Soon she found a job which she enjoyed. However, she insisted on working part-time so she would have the opportunity of visiting her family back in Nebraska. Although she had kept in close touch with her children by phone, the opportunity to visit her sons and the rest of her family contributed substantially to her well-being. Each time she came back she had more energy to face the situation. The city appeared less threatening, and the Al-Anon group became a strong network of support. She began to take some courses in pottery—which had long been an interest of hers—and gradually built her skills into a successful small business.

Suddenly a crisis appeared. Mary Ann dropped out of college and was coming home. Lisa didn't know how she could cope with her daughter and was frightened that Mary Ann would find out about Richard's drinking. The therapist encouraged Lisa to stop covering up for Richard. She was to talk frankly to Mary Ann, explain about her father's illness and steer the daughter to deal with her father directly. Lisa did so. She also invited Mary Ann to come to a session with the therapist, but her daughter decided not to. Lisa handled this problem successfully on her own.

Overall, a new pattern developed in the spouse unit of this family. Lisa detached herself from her husband's drinking but not from Richard as a husband. With no intention of separating, she simply accepted his illness. They went to church together and had an active social life. When Richard had had too much to drink, Lisa would insist they leave the car and take a cab home. When he drank excessively, she would leave him alone, but she made sure that his meals were prepared. When he passed out at dinner or other times and she had to leave the house to go to a meeting or a class, she made sure that no cigarettes were left burning and he was comfortably perched, but did not let that interfere with her own plans.

The therapist urged Lisa to invite Richard to join in their sessions. According to Lisa, he simply refused. Apparently Richard understood that he was an alcoholic, but he saw no reason to stop drinking. It was not interfering with his job, and he had no sense that he was neglecting his family. Lisa accepted his denial. She decided to continue working on herself and building up her own life, freeing Richard to do as he pleased.

Lisa did take several of the steps I suggested to make sure Richard stayed in contact with his children. She made a point of calling their sons whenever Richard was available to talk with them. Mary Ann had settled in an artist's colony in Chicago, and she also kept in close contact by phone, particularly whenever she needed money. Lisa always referred Mary Ann to her father. In the past, she had probably acted as a go-between for her husband and children. Now she carefully began to remove herself from that role, so that Richard would have a stronger sense of playing a needed role within his family.

Through individual therapy, Lisa McCarthy built up a life for herself that included a dysfunctioning husband. She accepted the problems as something that would continue, just as she accepted alcoholism as a chronic illness from which Richard would suffer for the foreseeable future. Not only did she teach herself to see Richard as a sick person and accept that without resentment, she also helped the children and the extended family see him in the same way. She was functioning well and so was her family, and Lisa was satisfied with that.

How would his case be evaluated therapeutically? From Lisa's point of view, therapy was successful. Personal gratification through new interests and maintaining a well-functioning family were sufficient to compensate for the stresses of living with an active alcoholic.

The ideal of a recovered alcoholic living happily within a changed family system cannot always be achieved. In the McCarthy case, the failure to reach Richard did not change the fact that Lisa's functioning improved greatly through therapy, as did the functioning of the family network.

The Stewarts

Failure in work performance is often an important factor in motivating an alcoholic toward treatment. This was true for Peter Stewart, who committed himself to the A.A. program, sobered, and maintained his recovery. But when the family functioning does not improve, due to another member's alcoholism, there will still be adverse effects.

Both parents in the Stewart family were alcoholics and had been since their teens. Peter was a factory maintenance worker; Emily was a housewife; they had two children.

In his early thirties Peter Stewart hit a particularly bad period, and for the first time his drinking began to affect his job performance seriously. Increasing absenteeism and poor performance when at work caused his supervisor to refer him to the factory's employee health services. The counselor there confronted Peter Stewart with his heavy drinking, suggested that he be detoxified, and put him in touch with A.A. Peter followed through with these suggestions. He committed himself to the A.A. program. His drinking stopped, and he began to recover. His job performance also improved. However, he felt his wife's alcoholism threatened his recovery and left the household. He could see his life changing, and he was delighted. The counseling service closed the case; prognosis: promising.

But an important area of Peter's life remained unchanged: his family life. Eight months after his first referral, he called the counselor again. This time his concern was for Emily, still an active alcoholic, and his children, particularly his son, Marty (12), who had been involved in some minor delinquency "because of the influence of bad friends."

Employee counseling services are designed to focus on helping the individual and on improving the individual's work performance. But Peter Stewart's counselor realized that the functioning of the individual on the job and elsewhere cannot help but be affected when his or her family is in difficulty. He referred Peter Stewart to a family therapist.

The family therapist's first contact with Mr. Stewart was by phone. The case record stated that he had been working on his drinking, and that his current concern was his wife and son. Mr. Stewart explained that his wife Emily, who had like himself been an alcoholic since her teens, had been trying to sober up through A.A. and other services since her husband had stopped drinking, but she had not succeeded.

Knowing that Mrs. Stewart was drinking, but not knowing how intoxicated she might be, the therapist then made plans to see the couple without the two children.

When the couple came to the session, Emily had just attained three days of sobriety. She was pleased to be sober, but her appearance showed long neglect of herself. Her hair was dyed blond but it had not been done for so long that it was a combination of blond and brown. Her face was red and swollen. Her eyes were bloodshot, and she was hiding her body with her arms and a too-tight jacket, which she refused to take off. Mr. Stewart, in contrast, was nicely dressed in a short-sleeved shirt and a neat pair of slacks. He looked so well that even though he was also in his late thirties, he looked ten years younger than his wife.

The couple did not meet each other's eyes. It was very difficult for them to face each other or the therapist. But they were there with a common concern; their children, and Peter's concern for another human being suffering from alcoholism.

The couple session focused on Emily and how she would handle her drinking problem. The therapist assured them that Marty's problems would also be focused on during therapy. But alcoholism was such a core problem in this family that nothing could be achieved until this had been dealt with. The plan initially was to help Emily deal on an individual basis with her drinking. Peter could not help her because his own sobriety was still threatened. They could easily have fallen back into the old pattern of this family system, with Peter acting as husband and father—but also as drinking partner.

Emily explained that she had committed herself to the A.A. 90-day program. Peter was very supportive of her efforts, and he promised to drive her to A.A. meetings. They talked about the children, and Peter said again that he was concerned about Marty. Marty had been unjustly blamed for the theft of a bike. He was a very shy and non-aggressive child who couldn't defend himself. The couple was reassured that a session including the children was planned for the following week, but since it was obvious that Emily's mind was not entirely clear, any further exploration of issues in this session was inadvisable. The therapist told Emily to keep in touch with her by phone. A time was arranged for Emily to call the therapist each day, to report on her doings. This is a therapeutic technique that supports the A.A. philosophy of staying sober one day at a time. During the week, Emily called the therapist faithfully. She felt encouraged and supported, and she was looking forward to coming to the next session with the children.

Emily succeeded in maintaining sobriety. The therapist knew this, but she was amazed at the changes already apparent at the next session. Emily was nicely dressed, her face had returned to normal, and her mind was clear. It was obvious that Emily was already anxious to be seen in her recovering state—an excellent sign of progress.

Tina, age 8, was dressed like a 15-year-old, in high heels and panty hose. Her behavior, too was that of a little lady. She smiled all the time. Marty, like his father, was very much dressed up for this session, but he seemed more his age. Both children were very shy.

When we started to discuss family problems, Marty at the beginning was mute. Tina, with some prompting, admitted that there were problems; then she smiled again, and she could not really say what they were. The closest she could come was to talk about their house, neglected now because her father wasn't there. Things were breaking down, and there was no one to fix them. She looked at her father, but said no more.

Emily too had difficulty describing her needs. She said actually there was little trouble, and that both children were doing well. The therapist allowed silence to fall. Then Emily admitted that Marty was not doing so well in school. He would like his father to help him, she said, but his father wasn't there. Since she was not as well-educated as her husband, she could not help Marty with his homework.

Marty remained very quiet. The therapist tried to reach him by chatting about his interests. Marty said he didn't participate in after-school activities. He had to come straight home, pick up his bike, do the shopping, then come back to help his mother. The therapist asked about supper. Both children smiled and said that was no problem; they both knew how to do hamburgers and frozen fries.

A picture of the family began to develop. Mr. Stewart, understandably concerned about the effects his wife's drinking might have on his own sobriety, had been avoiding the house. Emily's drinking had worsened. As a result, the children had been neglected and badly affected by their parents' problems. Both of them were taking on adult roles in order to help their mother, and Tina showed the pseudo-maturity often seen in

alcoholics' children. Though Marty longed to join the
adolescent peer group, he was so desperate for friends that he
allowed himself to be the goat of the neighborhood toughs. He
was also experimenting with pot.

It was important at this point to give this family the sense
that they were working for change. The therapist suggested
continuing with couple sessions, in which Peter and Emily
could work on functioning as a parental team. Combined with
these would be sessions including the children, which would
focus on actual parental issues. The therapist would also
continue seeing Emily individually, to support her individual
needs. Close contact by phone would continue; Emily would
need a lot of support to build up her sobriety. The family
agreed.

A third goal, not yet to be discussed with the family, was to
work with Peter and Emily as spouses. In this strategy the
therapist was following Minuchin's paradigm of the family as a
system differentiated into spouse and parental subsystems.
Peter and Emily were both concerned parents, anxious to help
their children. But they had both been alcoholics for the entire
twelve years of their married life. All the tasks of spouse
subsystem formation had been handicapped, and probably
overshadowed, by drinking. If there was any problem in their
sexual relationship, it would have been ascribed to drinking.
Learning how to read each other and support each other had
obviously been impossible. Patterns for negotiating and
resolving conflict had not developed. If Peter and Emily were to
build a relationship as spouses—and their ability to do this
remained to be seen—they would have to start from scratch.

After a few sessions, the Stewarts began to get in touch with
their needs and expectations of each other. Emily was afraid of
saying too much. She was still unsure of her sobriety, and she
would not express her needs, or what she wanted from her
husband. But after she had celebrated her 90 days of sobriety in
A.A., she began to feel stronger. She started to talk about her
needs. She definitely wanted Peter to take over some parental

tasks—the children needed their father. But it was obvious that she felt considerable ambivalence about having him back in the house. She simply did not know how to relate to this man as a husband, in a relationship that did not include drinking. Furthermore, the Stewarts had been separated for almost a year, and during that year there had been little contact between them. Emily felt confused and unsure about the role of wife, and it was obvious that much work in this area would be necessary.

When summer came, the family began to talk about a vacation. The therapist seized on this as an opportunity for expanding the family experience. Emily had been taking over more and more of the household chores. Both Marty and Tina, though pleased at her increasing competence, sensed an empty space in their lives, left by giving up the responsibilities they had carried. They both needed to develop age-appropriate interests. Marty, in particular, was still far too shy, coming to life only when he discussed his hobby: geography. The therapist arranged summer camp for the children. They were also referred to Alateen.

Both Peter and Emily were doing very well on their recovery, and slowly, Peter was growing closer to his family. They planned a family weekend at the beach and carried it through successfully. The children were delighted.

During the summer, the apartment Peter was sharing with another man had to be given up. The couple agreed that he should move back home, but this presented great problems for them both. The therapist worked with them intensively, helping Peter re-enter the household and family, and helping the couple deal together with the children on a day-to-day basis. Peter began to work on the falling plaster and broken linoleum, and slowly the couple began to work together on other tasks. They could no longer use drinking as the escape from and excuse for all problems, but they were willing to face the difficulties of building a relationship as husband and wife.

The favorable prognosis for the Stewart family is based partly on the strengths inherent in this family, particularly the parents' determination to help their children before early signs of difficulty worsen. Their ability to keep themselves sober and remain closely involved with A.A. also gives hope that changes can be accomplished.

Chapter Three

Five Women Affected by Alcoholism

"It was my fault, it was my fault, Bartley," she sobbed...
"Well, don't cry, don't cry! It wasn't altogether your fault,"returned
Bartley. "We were both to blame." "No! I began it. If I hadn't
broken my promise about speaking of Hannah Morrison, it never
would have happened..."
"Oh, well, never mind about it; don't take on so," coaxed Burtley.
"It's all over now, and it can't be helped. And I can promise you," he
added, "that it shall never happen again, no matter what you do..."
W.D. Howells: A MODERN INSTANCE

Alcoholism is a disease classically focused on the individual
male alcoholic, shutting out the "other victims" of alcoholism.
Now we are beginning to recognize the wives and daughters of
alcoholics as a large population who may have suffered every
degree of mental and physical cruelty. Perhaps worse, they are
trapped in interactional patterns which confine them to the role
of "alcoholic's wife."

"I knew I shouldn't be able to sleep, I was so mad at you "
"Oh!"

"And I dropped into the hotel barroom for a nightcap—for something to make me sleep..."
W.D. Howells: *A MODERN INSTANCE*

This chapter describes a group of women I met through individual, couple, family, and/or group therapy. Four of them had married alcoholics. The fifth was unable to separate sufficiently from her alcoholic family of origin to establish a life of her own. All were depressed and angry, and, characteristically, these women had difficulty seeing themselves as individuals—people in their own right—with their own needs and goals. They seemed to have no role in life other than being victims of alcoholism. Even in therapy, their individual needs and desires had been subordinate to the needs of the alcoholic. They were seeking therapy to find support in bearing their pain, not to free themselves as individuals.

The married women in this group were in their thirties and forties. All of them were well-educated and doing well in their careers. None was alcoholic. Most of them, as is not uncommon among wives of alcoholics, were overweight. All of them had conflicts with their sexuality and several presented homosexual fears. All of them were highly skeptical about the possibility of establishing healthy relationships with men and thought they lacked the attributes necessary for good experiences as women. Intensely aware that they had gotten themselves into relationships with alcoholics, they were terrified of repeating the same mistakes in forming future relationships.

These women had another factor in common which promptly came to the front in therapy. They were all still closely involved with their families of origin and, interestingly enough, four of them had alcoholic parents.

Although statistics have never been gathered, a growing body of anecdotal material suggests that this syndrome is not uncommon: wives of alcoholics, like alcoholics themselves, tend to come from families affected by alcoholism. In the case of the alcoholics themselves, this may be partly hereditary. But why should their wives, who may often refuse to drink, have entered into union with them? We are beginning to learn how traumatic the effects of parental alcoholism can be for children, particularly in regard to their development of sex and role identity. It may be that the daughters of alcoholics grow up in an environment so skewed they never appreciate that other options are open to them. They learn to live primarily as adjuncts to alcoholism. And this is the life they establish for themselves in their marriages.

The Group

This group was formed out of the planned ending of an earlier women's group. The members of the first group were women in their fifties and sixties. One was married to an active alcoholic, another to an intermittent alcoholic, and another to a man who had stopped drinking but began abusing other drugs. In late middle age, these women were not set to effect many changes in their lives beyond finding ways to accommodate to the reality of coping with their husbands' addiction.

When Irene, a woman of 37, came to the therapist for marital therapy, the therapist suggested she join this women's group. Irene became a group member, though very passive and quiet, for a short time. When the group agreed to stop meeting, Irene wanted to continue. The therapist was in the process of beginning a group with younger women. Irene joined this and, as the "old timer," she quickly became the group leader.

But the therapeutic focus for this second group was different. These younger women wanted to create a life of their own. If they could manage within their marriages, they would, but if not, they would go it alone. Group rules were different from the former group. Support was combined with confrontation—a new experience for the group members who were involved with Al-Anon.

Wives of alcoholics have a great need of support, and in group situations they tend to provide this support to each other by protecting, denying and/or cheering up. As a result, such a group can sometimes become unhealthy—comforting, but static. Some Al-Anon members learn a pattern of immediate gratification: when you feel pain, you are to call another member, tell her about it, and she will comfort you. When these patterns began to emerge in this group, the therapist firmly confronted these tendencies and steered the women to acknowledge their problems and work them through. They were to look closely into what aspects of their lives were worth change. Furthermore, they were not encouraged to keep in touch outside of the group context. If a crisis came up, they were to call the therapist, with the option of sharing their experiences with the group later on, if they wished. Pain was alleviated in the group, but not with the immediate comfort which becomes an end in itself.

The results of this orientation were positive. These women had to learn to know themselves, as people. The overriding themes in the group were anger, depression, and self-worth. Eventually, they all became very open, giving warmth and support, and were able to experience the closeness they needed in the group. But for a long time they had difficulty confronting each other in the attempt to deal with core issues— their anger, sexuality, and what they would do to make their lives better.

Irene

When Irene came to the therapist for marriage counseling she was 37, of medium height, quite thin, with hair straggling to her shoulders making her small face look like a caricature of a mannequin. She had had individual therapy before, so she immediately began to report the details she assumed the therapist wanted. Her mother had died of alcoholism, and her father had committed suicide shortly afterward. She had a married sister, seven years younger, with whom she kept in sporadic contact. She never heard any more from her brother. A native of Nova Scotia, she had left her family in her early 20's to come to New York to study art, but an accident had injured the nerves in her right hand, and she'd had to give up painting. She worked now as an administrative assistant and considered herself very competent in her job.

Irene cried when she talked about her parents' deaths, but she also assured the therapist that she had already mourned them. What she wanted now was help with her marriage.

Irene said that her husband was an Ivy League graduate, "very intellectual," but in an advanced stage of alcoholism. He would sober up, get a job, and maintain both for two to three weeks. Then he would begin drinking again. She had gone to some Al-Anon meetings, but she didn't like the group of women there. She recognized their anger and their inability to face it or work on it, which she found extremely depressing.

The therapist saw Irene and her husband. He was a "nice guy" type, very intellectual, as she said, but tight-lipped, and divorced from his feelings. The only way Irene could arouse any reaction from him was by yelling and screaming. He would make no commitment to work on his drinking or go to A.A. So the therapist decided to see Irene on an individual basis and also suggested that she join the first women's group.

With the older women, Irene was the silent member; she would share her feelings only if specifically called upon. As she began to trust the other group members, she became more active, and when the second group was formed, she quickly took a leading role. She was the confronting one, actively using the group to her benefit for learning about her feelings and expressing them. She decided not to mention her husband in the group. The group was for her, and specifically for dealing with the unresolved conflicts about her dead parents and gaining courage from the other group members to explore these issues.

Irene was very angry with her mother; she felt she had never had a mother available to her. Thus, she couldn't see her mother as a person, but only the alcoholic she was. In terms of her father, she was also angry because, as is typical, she blamed him for her mother's drinking. She liked her younger sister, but didn't want to know anything about her brother.

One of the other women in the group reminded Irene of her mother. In the group sessions, she began to work out some of her repressed feelings. For the first time, she was able to express her anger verbally. As she became aware of herself and her feelings, she also began to remember how much she had actually gotten from her mother. It was this woman who had given her some of the positives she was beginning to discover in herself, especially her ability to organize and a great capacity for caring about people.

The area Irene couldn't begin to work on yet was her anger toward men. At one time the therapist suggested bringing two men into the group. Irene refused to accept the idea. She wasn't ready. Still too angry to deal with men, she needed to work on herself as a woman first.

Irene's husband was drinking more and more. As his condition deteriorated, he was abusing her both physically and mentally. She felt unable to abandon him, but finally he left her. That created the opportunity to reorganize her life, and she developed a small network of friends, an impossible task when she was married and her husband actively drinking. She began attending Al-Anon sessions again, accepting as useful some of the philosophy of the program. She had good

experiences relating to some of the women there; she was
meeting people she could trust.

During this period she had a short affair with one man in his
40's and a longer affair with a younger man, proving to herself
that she could still function sexually, and that she was not the
frigid woman she had once thought. But she continued being
very angry, especially at the parents who had "left her."

Irene had never gone back home and had never been to her
parents' graves. The group encouraged her to make a trip back,
get in touch with her brother, visit her sister, and visit her
parents' graves. Eventually, Irene did go home, but upon
visiting her brother, discovered that he was an alcoholic. When
Irene came back she was furious with the entire group,
particularly the therapist, because her visit had been so painful
for her. She dealt directly with her anger at the therapist in the
group. The group had never seen her angry, and some of them
were frightened at her drastic loss of control. However, the
therapist encouraged Irene to continue relating her experience
of visiting her parents' graves and reliving her early years,
pointing out that she understood how painful this must have
been. With the support of the group and therapist, Irene was
able to work through her anger. She had to accept the fact that
her parents were dead and that she must now work on a life of
her own. Much later, she told of a dream: she was in an
Al-Anon meeting and met her mother, who asked, "When are
you going to leave me in peace?" Irene took this as a message
that she must stop blaming her mother for what was going on
with her and start taking responsibility for her own life.

At around this time another member, Miriam, was meeting
with her parents and working through some of her own
conflicts with them. The experiences Miriam described in the
group helped Irene a lot because she was experiencing similar
feelings, fantasizing sessions or contacts with her parents where
she could resolve the conflicts she had never worked through
with them. Eventually it grew easier for Irene to deal with her
conflicts, and she returned home and visited with her brother

and sister several times. Once she sent the therapist a postcard from Canada, showing a father tiger guarding his mate and cubs.

Physically, Irene has grown softer and much more feminine in her appearance. She sports a stylish haircut and wears attractive, sexy clothing. Her confidence has increased. Once she managed to face her bosses with a demand for the promotion she knew she deserved, and got it.

Irene's husband stopped drinking after their separation and has maintained sobriety. Irene keeps in touch with him, but never mentioned him in the group. The group was her means of working on herself, her own identity and growth.

Miriam

Like the other married women in this group, Miriam, 30, came to therapy originally for marital counseling. The first session was with the couple. Miriam wore a hat and a sheepskin coat that hid her body completely. She was quite overweight. Her husband, a young man, looked very pale and was extremely quiet—a stoneface. A chronic alcoholic, he had been sober through A.A. for a year, but otherwise showed marked signs of emotional dysfunction. He was almost impossible to reach, showing no enthusiasm or interest in anything.

They took seats at opposite ends of a long couch. Miriam was depressed and tearful. Her husband just sat. There seemed to be no contact between them, and the therapist could sense no flow in their relationship. This pattern remained unchanged for three or four sessions, the husband not making himself available to changes and Miriam's depression deepening. Temporary separation was recommended, and the couple agreed.

Like other husbands of the women in the group, John was largely supported by his wife. He was a free-lance editor who got work only intermittently. However, at this point in his life, and sober, he was probably pleased that somebody else had made this decision for him, and he managed to get a room and move out of the couple's apartment.

Once separated, Miriam turned to her parents for support. Hers was a suburban Jewish family she had come back to very rarely since leaving for college. After the separation, she began visiting often. The parents fussed and took care of her, and she again experienced support, both emotionally and financially. Her mother took her out to buy clothes, often purchasing the same outfit for herself. Her father slipped her spending money. But very soon Miriam became their go-between, and she noticed how they resorted to talking about and to each other through her, just as they always had. Father would say, "Your mother told me that you told her..." Mother would say, "You had better be careful with your father today, because he doesn't feel well." Miriam was falling into her old role of dependent teenager. Away from her parents, she was a competent woman with her own successful business. At home, she was "Mimi" again.

Watching her father, after her experience with an alcoholic husband, Miriam made a discovery. For the first time, she realized that her father was a "functioning alcoholic." As a terrified child, running to hide when he began to yell and throw things, she had never labeled the problem. Now she realized that those fits of abuse occurred when he had had too much to drink.

A second discovery was to realize that they were keeping her dependent. Her mother became more openly controlling, and her father (who had set her up in her business) was using money to maintain close contact. At that point, she requested a session together with her parents. There were three family sessions altogether. Miriam was in a hysterical stage, yelling and screaming, telling her parents to let her be independent and at the same time begging for closeness. Her parents couldn't really listen. They could only see the "crazy" daughter they felt sorry for, who must be controlled for her own good.

But the sessions were important for Miriam, not only because she was able to ventilate some of her feelings, but also because she began to realize that her parents could not hear her. She began to understand that she must separate from her parents and move beyond her anger as well as her child-role of go-between. Only then would she be able to go back to them as a mature woman and be accepted that way.

She began to work on this in individual sessions, which she paid for with her own money. Her chief concern in these sessions was still her family. She tried to get closer to her sister, Rachel, who suffered from severe asthma and wanted to bring her in to therapeutic sessions. Rachel was closely involved with their mother (who, incidentally, bore the main responsibility for taking care of Rachel's children), and she decided not to come to sessions, afraid these would upset her. Miriam acquiesced in Rachel's decision, not wanting that responsibility.

One session was held with Miriam and her father. Miriam prepared herself for days, planning to really tell him off, venting years of anger. But in the session, she was astonished to find herself talking to a different person. This was not the harsh father she had always feared. This was a gentle man capable of great warmth, and Miriam was amazed. He had never been able to show this side to his family. The therapist questioned the change: why was he so different? He said his wife overpowered them all, allowing him only one role in his family: the provider.

Miriam never told her father she had planned to tell him off. It was much more pleasant to get in touch with a side of him she had never seen. After the session, she planned ways she could get to know her father better.

As Miriam became more aware of herself, the therapist suggested that she join the women's group. This would help her integrate her experiences with the experiences of women in similar situations. She agreed and immediately began working in the group on the issues of separating from her parents. Her experiences helped the others, encouraging them to do what she had had to do. In turn, the group was particularly helpful to Miriam in dealing with questions of her own sexuality and feminine role. Miriam felt an intense sense of failure as a woman. To her, a woman's role was to marry, bear children, and take care of husband and children. This was what her mother and sister had done; she was the only woman she knew well for whom marriage had not worked out. Even her successful business seemed another negation of femininity. If she went out with a man, she was careful never to mention her shop lest he would think her unwomanly and reject her immediately.

Now in group and individual sessions, Miriam began to gain self-confidence. She began to realize that she could have a successful business and be a woman, too. Work and success became a source of real gratification to her.

When the group discussed sexuality, Miriam confided that she felt she had been sexually abused by her husband, especially when he was drinking. She had no experience of pleasant sexual contacts with men, and she was afraid to try. She began to work on this area of her life very slowly. She had a few one-night affairs, trying to learn about herself, and gauge her readiness for relating to men. She also tried diets, diet pills, diet clubs, and Overeaters Anonymous. Through OA she began to lose pounds and finally reached a normal weight. She began to understand why she'd been using food; by eating and, as she said, "being fat," she'd kept men away from her. She began to study her body in the mirror. Gradually she learned to dress attractively instead of cloaking her body.

Miriam did manage to build enough security to let the feelings she had always pushed away come to the fore. No longer terrified of inadequacy, she was able to enjoy her new capacity for arousal. This was the last brick she needed for the structure she was building. Once this fit into place, she felt ready to terminate treatment.

Rose

Rose, an attractive black woman in her early 40s, was the only sober member of an alcoholic family. She was the pillar of her family, the one who took care of everybody. She worked to save money, then "lent" it to everyone. Her mother and siblings were actively drinking; her father was "on the street." As a girl she had combed the bars to find him and bring him home, but now, she said, she "couldn't care less." Her husband, from whom she had separated, was also an alcoholic. He lived in another city, but Rose managed to keep in touch with him through friends, and she was almost as involved with him as if they were still together, although they had been separated for two years. Rose came to therapy for help in reaching a decision regarding divorce. She thought the final decree would end her involvement with this man.

Rose was functioning well in a very responsible job in a research laboratory. She had been overweight, but had managed to trim down through a diet club. When she came to therapy she was living away from her family, whom she phoned and visited constantly, and with whom she was emotionally enmeshed. Intensely involved in a war with her mother, she found it impossible to express her anger at this woman. She had also become actively involved in Al-Anon, a source of support when she separated from her drinking husband. But what she learned she had never applied to her own family. She could see her husband as a sick person and pull away from him, but she couldn't do the same with her parents and siblings.

After a few individual sessions, the therapist suggested Rose join the group, and she agreed. In the first group session, Rose reiterated that she was coming to therapy to deal with her intention to divorce. But then she began to talk about her mother, who was coming to visit her the next day. Rose wanted her mother to be a perfect woman and could not accept her as a person with faults. She either blamed her for what she did, or wondered what she was up to. Rose complained that her mother would insist on cooking for her, keep her awake with her snoring, and generally make her life miserable.

The group focused on practical suggestions for the week, urging Rose to do what she could to enjoy her mother's stay. She should make arrangements for going out, or simply accept the fact that her mother enjoyed cooking for her, instead of deciding that her mother was trying to keep her a child. Rose was a mature woman. She was to relate to her mother like a mature woman, without feeling that she had to run away to defend herself.

Rose listened carefully, apparently quite happy to accept the group and the therapist as authority. Later, she said that the mother's visit marked the first time she had been able to understand that her mother was a human being, flawed like all humans, a person who snored. This theme recurred as she continued to perceive her mother's faults as those of a human being, instead of a nuisance directed towards her.

One of Rose's main problems was terror of her own anger. Irene's fury after her visit home was very frightening to Rose, who equated expression of anger with loss of control. One day only Irene and Rose attended a session. Irene provoked Rose, and Rose was able to express her anger. When she was finished, she couldn't believe that she had become angry without turning violent. Coming from an environment where almost every family member was alcoholic and expression of anger tended to be violent, she, the nonalcoholic, the good daughter, the controlled person, had been afraid that if she lost her temper, she might kill someone.

After this confrontation, Rose began to express some feelings toward her parents. The issue of divorce completely set aside, she began to work on resolving her conflicts with her parents. Once she started to perceive her mother as a person, she kept contact by long phone conversations and enjoyable visits. She tried hard to get in touch with her father, who was actively drinking When he had to be hospitalized for serious complications of alcoholism, she visited him, initiating contacts which continued. She talked with him, telling him where she was in her life. She tried to get close to her brother and sister, too, though their drinking made this very difficult.

Rose had many problems sexually. Sexually abused from an early age, she had been taught that sex was dirty. When sex was discussed in the group, she shared her experiences with masturbation but also her intense desire to live with a man so she could have sex. Most of the men she had relationships with were older white men. She talked about her need to be cared for like a child by these men and how much she had missed being cared for while growing up. Sometimes she would wonder if she was having incestuous relationships with men who reminded her of her father. As she began to work on understanding her feelings in therapy, she began to understand that she needed a different kind of man—a man who could relate to her as a woman, not a daughter, and take care of her in a different way.

At one point Rose developed a backache so serious that she was immobilized for nearly three weeks. No organic cause could be found. Rose confided to the group, very shyly, that she had called a spiritual healer. The healer told her that the pain was sent by her mother-in-law, who was upset that Rose had left her son. Rose had gotten out of bed immediately (she wasn't going to let her mother-in-law do that to her). Rose knew better, she said, than to confide this experience to her colleagues at the lab: "They'd lock me away." But the group did not criticize her. If those were her beliefs, she was entitled to them. To have the group accept her and not make fun of her was an intensely rewarding experience.

The group was useful to Rose as an experience of acceptance. To be able to share openly and be accepted was extremely important for her. She made great strides in understanding her family and also her current relationships with men. The group's acceptance of her and her beliefs helped her turn her energy to constructive channels. She plans to return to college to work for a degree.

Ellen

Ellen is an attractive woman born in Czechoslovakia just before World War II. Her father deserted her mother shortly after her birth, then was killed. Ellen never heard a good word about men. Her mother was a sour, bitter woman, powerful, but loading a lot of responsibility on her daughter. Ellen felt closer to her grandmother, who was a tender and loving woman. But the environment in which she grew up was rigid. She was punished, corrected, criticized, and constantly told she wasn't measuring up.

In her late teens Ellen moved away from home to look for a job in another city. There she got close to a group of lesbians, but she did not involve herself in a gay relationship with anyone. Friends suggested she come to America, where she found a job, and soon married a young man. He was an alcoholic, and in the early stage of her marriage she found herself abused sexually and mentally. At the age of 26, she joined Al-Anon, and came to the therapist for marriage counseling. After a few months of individual therapy and a very short experience in the first group of older women, she decided to separate from her husband, thinking that would resolve all of her problems. She stopped therapy, but she kept in touch with the therapist, sometimes calling on the phone when she felt she needed it, and she continued with Al-Anon meetings. At one meeting she told the therapist that her divorce had come through and her husband had left the city.

For the first time in her life, she was alone. But she was building a new life, and she told the therapist that she felt quite confident about herself and her capability.

A year later she called back. This time the problem she presented was her relationship with her mother across the ocean. Her grandmother had just died, and Ellen felt very responsible for her mother, "left alone in the old country." She was living with her mother's image. She couldn't enjoy going out, she couldn't enjoy being free, she couldn't even buy an outfit without hearing her mother's voice saying how bad and disloyal she was. She felt enormous guilt, both for having left her mother, and for having been so foolish as to marry an alcoholic. She had never even dared tell her mother that her husband was an alcoholic, since for Ellen and her family, alcoholism was a shameful thing. Now that she had separated she was able to work through her experiences with an alcoholic husband, mainly through Al-Anon. However, the problems with her mother remained. I suggested she join the second group.

The group helped Ellen understand two things. First, the bitterness of her childhood was largely due to the circumstances of wartime Europe. Second, she could not change her mother. She could only accept her, free herself from that relationship to become the person she wants to be, and deal with her mother as she actually is. The group helped her decide on a visit to her mother, which worked out quite well due to Ellen's determination not to challenge her mother's values or allow her mother to challenge hers.

Ellen had developed many serious problems on the job, mainly related to an inability to accept criticism from her colleagues because it conveyed painful images of her mother. Even positive criticism was to be rejected. She would come to the group and relate incidents at the office. The group, enriched by their own experiences, was instrumental in pointing out she was repeating her behavior with her mother in relating to her colleagues, and Ellen gradually began to recognize this fact.

At first Ellen wept frequently in meetings, usually when talking about her mother. But as she began to accept herself without feeling guilty, the crying lessened. She began to enjoy doing things, accepting the fact that she did not have to tell her mother every detail. Eventually she was able to plan weekend trips to friends in Europe, taking advantage of her job's travel privileges, and tell her mother about them, simply mentioning that she wasn't going to get to Czechoslovakia "this time."

Ellen was the most conservative woman in the group, uncomfortable discussing sexual issues. She still does not feel ready to commit herself to any long-term relationship. But she enjoys more casual relationships with men. Though a little overweight and "too busy with other things to bother about it," she dresses well and carries herself attractively. She seems increasingly able to accept herself and her identity.

Joanne

Joanne, 26, was the youngest woman in the group and the only unmarried member. She came to the therapist originally for individual treatment. She was very depressed and unable to get in touch with her feelings. She had had some superficial relationships with boys while in high school, but she had mostly hung around with her four brothers, as "one of the boys." Her mother was an active alcoholic. Her father had left the household. He kept in touch with the mother, checking on her safety, and paid the bills. But there was little else between them.

Joanne looked to the therapist as an authority, but it was almost impossible to break through her silences. Confronted with any problem, she would always agree. "Yes," she would say, "you are right. I have to work on that." And that would be the end of it. The therapist suggested that she join the second group.

Joanne agreed, but for some time she was silent, perhaps terrified, in meetings. It was hard to be sure she was even listening. The therapist tried to bring her in a few times by asking her to discuss the issue in relation to herself, but she couldn't relate any feelings to herself. One day she asked the therapist not to ask her to participate: the therapist was doing what her mother always did, and she resented it. And that was the end of her expressing any feelings for a while.

The group was very protective of Joanne. They never pushed her or confronted her, but they did make a point of contacting her nonverbally. Eventually this became a pattern. When an issue arose, one of the women, usually Irene, would smile at Joanne, and Joanne would respond with a very short sentence.

As the group opened up and the other women were able to share more openly their feelings, Joanne, more in touch with her own pain, became increasingly depressed. The only way she could show this was by crying like a child. Sometimes she tried to speak, but the words wouldn't come out. The therapist had to hug her and help her relax, cry, and recover from these crying stages.

When Miriam recounted her meetings with her parents, Joanne asked for a meeting with her father. She was beginning to get in touch with her anger, but she was still unable to express it. Father agreed and came for a session. He is the very image of the British major: rigid, unable to show feelings, but always lecturing. He expostulated his outrage that Joanne had lessened contact with him, and lectured about the proper relationship of daughters to their fathers. Joanne became the little girl being scolded; the only words she managed to get in were, "Yes, you are right." She was very disappointed and told of it to the group. They urged her to have a session with her mother.

Joanne felt this would be no use since her mother was actively drinking. But she agreed to try. The mother came to the session smelling of liquor, but she was not drunk. Joanne became a completely different person. This time she was the accuser. But the two women could not deal with their repressed feelings; they could only argue about facts related to Mother's drinking. She said plainly she wants to drink, was going to drink, and it's her sole business to decide. Joanne got quite angry, but she felt the satisfaction of at least being able to talk to her mother.

The therapist suggested that it would be valuable to see Joanne's role in her parents' relationship. This posed a considerable practical problem. Father would have to drive Mother into the city, and Joanne didn't know whether they

could be that close for that long a period. Nevertheless, they
managed it. Mother looked quite different. She had cut down
on her drinking in the interval, lost weight, and her face was
much less swollen. But the session was a repetition of the dyad
sessions. Father lectured and Joanne agreed to everything he
said. She argued about facts with Mother. The therapist did not
feel that much was accomplished because Father took control of
the session. The surfacing of significant feelings was not
allowed.

When Joanne discussed this with the group, they faced her
with the reality that her parents probably would not change.
She must accept that and begin building a life of her own. She
had been trying to get them together again, but this was futile,
and playing the good daughter would only keep her from
doing anything with her own life.

Joanne and Irene had established a very good rapport. Now
Irene was able to confront Joanne about her anger and her
difficulty in expressing it. Joanne related a few incidents at
work. Her bosses were a man and an alcoholic woman. With
the group's support and suggestions she started to deal with
them. She stood up to the man for the first time and
confronted the alcoholic woman with the fact that Joanne was
having to compensate for her poor performance. Joanne was
greatly pleased with this accomplishment. The group began to
point out that in trying to bring her mother and father
together, Joanne had kept herself in the middle of a triangle.
She was repeating this triangle endlessly with friends and
coworkers. Joanne began to learn to extricate herself out from
the middle, especially with friends.

She had a very difficult time when Irene left the group. She
still could not fully express her feelings, and instead she got
very angry with the therapist because she wasn't doing the job
for her. She got involved with a man and began to feel better.
But after three months of dating him she shared her doubts
about his drinking pattern with the group. As the group
discussed it, it became very clear that he was an alcoholic,

though in a functioning stage. Joanne was encouraged to confront him. The only thing she could manage was to call him on the phone and tell him he must choose between her and drinking. This was the last she heard from him. Again she went through a very painful time, unable to deal with the loss, and angry with the group because she had been forced to realize what was going on.

As the other women in the group began to find what they sought, group meetings were terminated by mutual agreement. Joanne continued in individual therapy, where some progress was made. She no longer becomes depressed to the point of being unable to function. She is able to feel comfortable with her mother. She talks to her, and visits her—a sign that she is detaching from her mother's alcoholism. She completely cut communication with her father, but she keeps in touch with her brothers. She is also exploring the possibility of changing careers, moving out of the helping profession she chose, in her continuing effort to find something for herself besides the role of helper. But it will be some time before she is able to continue without support therapy.

A Retrospective

The history of this group was a progression toward self-recognition and self-realization on the part of women whose development was severely handicapped by illness in their families of origin—in most cases, the illness of alcoholism. When they first entered therapy, it seemed they all saw themselves as appendages to alcoholism. The married women all sought help with their marriages; Joanne came for help with her mother's drinking.

Through working in the group, they began to function as people in their own right. Irene, Miriam, Rose and Ellen were all in the process of adjusting to separation and divorce. Rose and Ellen had already separated and Miriam had made the decision to do so, so it was easier for them. Significantly, both

Miriam and Ellen moved out of their apartments during the process of group therapy. They bought new furniture and decorated new places. Later Irene completely redecorated her apartment. New surroundings symbolized a fresh start for them, as "our place" became "my place." In each case a sense of autonomous worth began to develop, and these women began to exhibit in their personal lives the competence they had shown in the world of work.

These group members, although mature women, were still involved in many unresolved problems with their parents, many of which were related to one parent's alcoholism. They had to resolve problems of separation from their families of origin. They all, in some fashion, had to return to their families and work through the never completed process of growing from daughter into woman.

Finally, they all had to learn that they did have options. All of them were re-establishing, in their current lives, the patterns of families affected by alcoholism. By confronting each other with what they were doing, and working on their own self-actualization, they began establishing human relationships in which they could act as people, not appendages. They dealt with their anger and developed self-esteem. The changes in their lives were reflected in their actual appearance as well as their attitudes about themselves and others. By the end of treatment, these women who had been overwhelmingly depressed and angry would often leave a meeting giggling over some shared experience, instead of weeping in mutual misery and comfort-seeking.

I wrote the above in the form of a paper to be presented at a conference. When it was finished, I called each of the group members for an informal follow-up and suggested that we meet once, to pick up threads. They were pleased at the suggestion and came to see me and hear the paper. As I began to read the paper to them, I suddenly became aware that they had seated themselves in the order I had discussed them in the paper. At this follow-up meeting, I learned that Rose and Ellen had not been in touch with the other members of the group since they finished therapy. Miriam, Joanne and Irene, however, had become "close friends." Actually, they established a "social" relationship where Irene continued in a leadership role. This became clear a few days later when both Irene and Miriam requested to see me individually, for a few sessions. Irene, the more competent and mature woman was helping Miriam and Joanne understand unresolved conflicts.

Chapter Four

Tailoring Family Therapy to Alcoholic Families

> *...a teacher is supposed to speak in earnest terms and warn his disciple that the harmlessness and placidity of this moment are a mirage, that there is a bottomless abyss in front of him and that once the door opens there is no way to close it again!* Carlos Castaneda: **Tales of Power**

Well, as I was saying, I'd met a lot of the boys up in town this day, and they threw as many as two drinks into me; I know that for certain, because when we took the parting dose, I had a glass of whiskey in both my right hands, and had just twice as many friends as when I started. Henry Wallace Phillips: RED SAUNDERS

When you begin to think about alcohol and its uses and abuses, a whole range of human behavior is encompassed. The use of alcohol is intertwined with many significant emotional events: relaxation, heightening intimacy and enjoyment. There is the ritual use of alcohol in the Catholic and Jewish religions, and the equally venerable hard-drinking sailor who nevertheless is careful never to take a drink until the sun has sunk below the yardarm. There is the husband and wife who make a point of sitting down together for a quiet cocktail while the children set the table. There is the woman described by Peg Bracken as having her own personal gauge: with the first drink "she sees clearly how witty her friends are. On the second, she realizes how witty she is, herself. On the third, when she knows she is beautiful, too, she knows it is time to eat."—*I Try to Behave Myself*

> *One of the strangest things about heavy drinkers, me among them in those days, is that much that seems clear to you as you drink, in sober periods will never seem clear again, because of course it never was. Lillian Hellman: MAYBE*

Somewhere toward the middle of the spectrum, there are the many socially accepted behaviors which verge on danger. There is the three-martini business lunch so nearly obligatory that it has the blessing of the Internal Revenue Service. There is the cup of black coffee widely depended on to counteract the effects of three drinks before dinner. There is the equation of hard drinking with toughness, with creativity, with an enviable relaxation of conscious control. There is the collection of well-known personalities who have "come out" to relate their experiences with alcoholism, perhaps in a desire to help society improve its attitudes. We even see alcoholism advanced by prominent figures as an excuse or explanation for admittedly illegal or immoral acts.

Moving toward the at-risk end of the spectrum, we see the many individuals whose drinking is increasingly out of control. We find the weekend drinker who is beginning to overindulge on the commuter train as well. We find the man who drinks to

prove his manhood, who is reaching the point where he can
function neither with drinking nor without it. We find women
like Anina Giacomelli, the young like Jack O'Brien, and the old
like John Collins, who learn the hard way that alcoholism
makes no distinctions as to age, sex, race or creed.

By now most alcoholics can be accepted as sick people by
therapists, family and friends. They have learned that they can
reach out for help, and that alcoholics can be helped. But
helping individual men and women to become sober is not
enough if we don't also try to re-establish a new equilibrium
with the people who are involved with them. Current methods
of bringing about changes in the individual alcoholic are quite
advanced, but we still have a long way to go in helping their
families change an environment in which everything is
structured in response to active drinking in one or more family
members.

In this book, I tried to select cases that showed a variety of
people and problems. Some of the therapeutic strategies used
were successful, some were not. The alcoholic member varied
in different families. In some cases, therapy began with the
alcoholic family member; sometimes there was another point of
entry. I was working in different agencies, dealing with
different systems of professional people as well as different
groups of client families. Many groups are unrepresented in
this sampling. But I hope the reader will be able to derive the
principles of treatment with alcoholic families, which can then
be incorporated into his/her own therapeutic style and the
needs of a particular family.

I do want to emphasize: don't forget to treat the alcoholic.
And do not take it for granted that it will be easy to reach the
alcoholic family. Family systems resist change, however desired
change may be. This will test the therapist's strengths and
limitations to the utmost.

This book is not a syllabus of family therapy; you are only
sharing a therapist's experiences. Many years of study and good
supervision are necessary, and I am still learning with each new

family I see. I hope this book will awaken professional readers to the need to get the training to work with individual alcoholics as well as with their families. When you look into the individual in the context of the family, you will find your horizons widening to an extent that the mental health field is only beginning to explore.

When a family affected by alcoholism comes to therapy, therapeutic goals will differ according to each family's circumstances and wishes. Therapeutic strategies must be tailored to those individual-family goals, and to the needs and possibilities unique to this particular family group. There are, however, a few general principles which can help guide the therapist as he plans goals and methods for the individual family. A consideration of how these relate specifically to the alcoholic family is a useful way of sharpening our theoretical foundation.

Determining the Focus

In most cases, the most important step in reshaping abnormal behavior in the alcoholic family is to reach the individual alcoholic, helping him or her to overcome the drinking problem, attaining and maintaining sobriety. All the resources of individual therapy can be used in this endeavor, including psychotherapy, medical intervention, and/or referral to a therapeutic group or Alcoholics Anonymous. Any method which seems likely to be helpful in an individual case can be pursued within the context of a family orientation.

While the focus is on the individual alcoholic, the therapist must be careful not to reinforce the family assumption that their problem is his drinking. Human beings are trained—and possibly even structured—to think in terms of linear cause and effect. We want to know the cause of a phenomenon—or whom to blame. Most families come to therapy with an identified patient, whatever the presenting problem may be. In alcoholic families this human tendency is reinforced by the demonstrable underfunctioning of the alcoholic family member. In families where one of the executive members is a chronic alcoholic, the entire family structure may have been created "around" the alcoholic's underfunctioning. In other cases, the adaptation is more recent. But in either case, the family's formulation is the formulation of Mary and Gina Fitzpatrick: "Daddy is the problem. Help him, change *him*, and we'll be all right."

The actual situation is usually different. In most cases, alcoholism has become part of daily family life. All family members have adapted to the alcoholic's behavior, and many of the patterns which underpin the family structure are built around his drinking. As a result, the normal functioning of the alcoholic family helps to maintain drinking patterns.

Therefore, the transactional patterns that have formed around the alcoholic's disability must also be a target for change. The family will have to understand that therapy involves not only changing the alcoholic member, but also the faulty family organization. A family organization that permits the alcoholic to interact only as a handicapped person can only impede his recovery. The odds are good, too, that this family organization is also hampering the functioning of the "well" family members.

For simplicity's sake, let us postulate a temporal framework which may not, in fact, exist. The first step is to identify alcoholism as a problem and plan therapeutic steps toward overcoming alcohol abuse by the affected family member. The next is to define a therapeutic contract that covers pathogenic family patterns.

Sometimes the first step is easy. Alcoholism is the presenting problem, and therapy has been initiated by the alcoholic seeking help.

In other families alcoholism is hidden, and some other problem is the trigger that brings the family to therapy, as with the Richardsons. Sometimes the alcoholic herself is the index patient, but under another label, as with the Giacomellis. In either case, the therapist has to uncover and confront the family with one member's alcoholism.

Some therapists would focus on the presenting problem, reasoning that alcoholism may clear up as a result of change in the functioning of the family. In my experience, however, alcoholism is such a serious illness, and its impact on the family is so great, that little can be accomplished unless alcoholism is part of the therapeutic contract. This is particularly so when alcoholism is chronic in one of the executive family members. In some families with hidden alcoholism, however, the therapist does have to work with the presenting problem until a relationship of trust and hope has been established. At this point the contract becomes like that reached with families where alcoholism is the presenting problem: (1) focus on helping the alcoholic stop the drinking, making him responsible for it and by doing so removing alcoholism from its central place in the family; (2) at the same time target for change those family transactional patterns that are trapping all family members in growth-curtailing roles; (3) stimulate individual growth of family members which is *not* based on the family disability created by alcoholism.

In some families the therapist enters the family only after a long period of sobriety and sees old patterns still governing the family interaction. Even here we have to deal with the alcoholism because it is still part of the family life. This may be because the sobered alcoholic is overly involved with A.A., or because the nonalcoholic spouse is overly involved with Al-Anon, and they never integrated individual growth into family life. As with the Harrison and Williams families, the inertia of the family system has maintained patterns associated with the drinking years.

In any case, the focus is always the individual in his or her environment. Once a therapist has learned to think in systems terms, any other focus is recognized as incomplete. This is true even when a contract for family treatment is impossible, as with the O'Briens and the McCarthys. Individual treatment helped

Jack O'Brien and Lisa McCarthy *vis a vis* their families, helping them escape from the roles they had been carrying out.

Family Assessment
Therapy with alcoholic families will generally involve an assessment of three areas (again this is imposing a time frame which may not exist). The therapist must be aware of the stage of alcoholism, the stage of family development and any cultural factors important for this particular family.

The stage of alcoholism will usually be analyzed by getting a good history and by observation. It will often be important to correlate this with family developmental stages. The older Giacomelli boys, for instance, escaped much of the impact of Anina's alcoholism. By the time her drinking became a problem, they were already separating from their mother in age-appropriate fashion.

Many families with a functional alcoholic are already in therapy, and these families are generally easier to restructure. Drinking can be dealt with on an outpatient basis, and it will be easier to move the alcoholic back into a more functional role within the family. Advanced alcoholism must be dealt with more drastically—with hospitalization, rehabilitation, etc., and work with that family will encounter a much more developed alcoholic family pathology.

The use of alcohol is so pervasive and so accepted in our culture, that the therapist will often run into a "how many times is normal" dilemma in assessing the role of alcohol in a family. In some families, quite heavy drinking is accepted as the norm. Some wives simply expect their husbands to stop by the bar on payday, arriving home late but relaxed. "All men drink—so what?" Sometimes, however, a therapist picks up warning signs of trouble that the family is not yet articulating. "He spends the whole afternoon watching football" may translate as, "I'm alone all week because he's at work, and on the weekends I'm still alone because he's dozing off in front of

the television after four beers." Children may complain that
Dad never helps them with their homework any more, which
may translate as, "Every evening after dinner he goes off to the
den to watch TV, next to his well-stocked executive's portable
bar." Sometimes a therapist can pick up signs of inappropriate
compensation—the mother gives the kids money to go to the
movies *every* Saturday, because Father is not going to be
available for family activities. "We never take trips any more...";
"He always used to help with the groceries..."; "He's usually
late for dinner these days..."; all may indicate that the normal
problems of families are becoming exacerbated by worsening
problem drinking.

The stage of family development can be analyzed by any of
several systems. Minuchin's is particularly useful in
pinpointing areas of therapeutic concern. With the Harrison
family, for instance, the family developmental stage dictated the
concentration on the spouse subsystem. The children were
growing up and leaving home; and, in fact, it was Clara's
perception of the need to rebuild the spouse subsystem that
brought the Harrisons into therapy.

Often, too, the idea of stages can help delineate areas for
repair. Alcoholic families in general have some "griefwork" to
do. They have a sense of loss, especially when they compare
themselves to the normal American family, with its husband,
wife, and 2.2 children, eternally problem-free and happy. They
often have to be encouraged to build on what they have,
without dwelling on what they missed in the past.

Freddie Harrison, at the age of 19, had barely known his
father. Becoming aware of this through therapy, Fred was able
to move toward his son, forming a new subsystem within the
family that let the men relate to each other without the
intermediation of Clara or Mary. There was no "turning the
clock back." Fred was able to talk with Freddie only because he
was able to accept his son as an adult. But the realization that
his son still needed his father and could be reached now, in the
present, was important for both of them.

In a few cases, it may be possible to turn back the clock. Audrey's mother was an alcoholic for years. Audrey took on the duties of parental child, rearing her younger sister, taking on the cooking and ultimately managing to graduate from college with high honors while carrying most of the responsibility for the household. During Audrey's junior and senior years in college, her mother committed herself to stop drinking and succeeded. Seeing the family in exploratory sessions, I recognized the familiar pseudomature, overachieving parental child pattern and encouraged Audrey, now 22, to "take a year off." Instead of accepting the high-pressure job she'd been offered, Audrey bought a car and began a trip across the country, something she'd always wanted to do. Taking an apartment of her own, she began to experiment with a variety of boyfriends, refusing to become serious about anyone while she was having her fling.

Taking off on an impulse trip, she found herself marooned in another city. She called me collect to ask what she should do. Recognizing the signs of an adolescent fling, I told her to call her mother. Audrey did, and her mother wired the money for gas to get her home.

Audrey stayed with her mother for a week while her mother cooked for her, did her laundry, scolded her, and in general made a fuss over her, something she had never done during Audrey's childhood. In effect, Audrey was able to be a teenager at the age of 22, giving herself a vacation from the constraints of her real adolescent years. She was able to experience herself as a daughter and a teenager, instead of as a responsible adult. Soon she was able to begin relating to her mother as one adult to another adult.

The idea of family stages is useful in therapy, but within certain limits. It is tempting to follow the paradigm too closely, letting one's thinking start with the spouse unit, then move to the parental team. I think now that an exaggerated focus on the spouse unit caused me to underattend Carmela Giacomelli. Family circumstances, too, make generalization difficult. It is not always possible to start with the spouse unit. The Williams and the Stewarts were able to relate to each other only as parents. It took many weeks of concentration on parental issues before they could begin to think of dealing with matters of spouse intimacy.

The third major area of family assessment is the cultural background, which may well dictate goals and techniques foreign to the therapist's own experience. For example, one of the premises of Minuchin's family developmental model is the importance of delineating the boundaries protecting the spouse unit from the extended family. With the Fitzpatricks, however, a couple of Irish and Italian backgrounds, helping them relate more closely with each family of origin was a vital factor in improving the spouse relationship.

One of Sarah and Shlomo's worst problems was cultural shame. Brought up to believe the myth that Jewish culture somehow protects from the dangers of alcoholism, Sarah made heroic efforts to keep Shlomo's "affliction" a secret from their extended family and friends, while continually nagging Shlomo to "do something about it."

When she was 36, Sarah came to me for help in coping with her alcoholic husband and rearing their daughter, Rachel, 14. She warned me that Shlomo would never hear of coming to therapy. He simply refused to accept having a problem with drinking. How could a Jew be an alcoholic? I began to work with Sarah and Rachel, helping them accept that alcoholism can affect even devout Jews; I encouraged them to concentrate on their own interests and growth and detach from Shlomo's drinking. A few months after the initiation of therapy, I got a phone call from Shlomo: he wanted to see me. We discussed his drinking problem, and he said, with a good deal of anger, that he'd had to come to see me because, for the first time, he was "feeling guilty" about his drinking. Since Sarah had stopped nagging him about it, he had no one but himself to blame for it. The changes Rachel brought into the family made him feel responsible for his drinking and ready to enter therapy. He learned to accept alcoholism as an illness. The most difficult issue to be dealt with in the future would be explaining why he could not drink wine during the Passover Seder.

Interventive Techniques

I have tried in this book to apply known theoretical principles of family therapy to families with alcoholism. As with matters of family assessment, there are no certain applications of intervention techniques specific to families with alcoholism.

"Joining" is developing the fundamental human relationships that make one individual feel validated by another. If clients do not feel valued by the therapist who is trying to change what they are accustomed to, therapy will be impossible.

Every member of an alcoholic family must feel the therapist's acceptance, including the alcoholic. Therefore, a therapist must be aware of her own reactions toward heavy drinking. If the therapist cannot accept the concept of alcoholism as an illness, she won't be able to teach the family that concept.

The ability to convey hope is vital to work with alcoholic families. Alcoholic families tend to be depressed and despairing. They have gone through years of struggle, and, in their eyes, they have failed. It is difficult for them to believe that anything can really improve. They will come to therapy in the same spirit that they have done everything else—to help the alcoholic. But they will not really believe that life can be better for them unless the therapist is able to convey that hope.

The therapist must also be respectful of the family. I am always wary of fitting every family into a mold. I recommend an initial therapeutic contract that calls for at least two, and better, three sessions. During these sessions, I keep a low profile, trying to let the family do its thing and through it learning about this family. It is important to convey hope and to establish oneself as the leader. But it is more important to see how these particular people think and interact.

A therapist must be on guard, too, against her own biases— on alcohol and other issues in life. A woman whose ambitions in life are centered around the role of the perfect housewife will probably conflict with those of a female mental health professional. But if that is the woman's goal, as with Anina Giacomelli, the therapist should respect it.

Techniques of changing an alcoholic family nearly always involve restructuring boundaries in a way that will allow the alcoholic back in. We do it by rebuilding the spouse subsystem and the parental subsystem, making room for the alcoholic, and helping provide compensation for whatever family members are displaced by the new arrangement.

We help people move into new positions, but, again, while doing all that, we have to be careful. Where there has been a parental child, for instance, therapy will usually involve freeing that child from inappropriate responsibilities. But a parental child is not *ipso facto* at risk. It is often appropriate to get the family working as a team, rather than appointing one parent the slave.

Diana is in her second year of sobriety. Deserted by her husband, an active alcoholic, she moved in with another man, also an alcoholic, who comes and goes. Diana's children are 15, 12 and 10. She also has a small daughter by her lover and is again pregnant.

The 15-year-old functions as a substitute father, but all the children have clearly defined roles in the household. The 12-year-old is responsible for the laundry and taking out the garbage. The 10-year-old helps in the kitchen, and the 3-year-old sets the table. A group of young professionals watching this family during a session reacted strongly against this arrangement. They felt the mother should be doing the housework, leaving the children free. But the two women in the group who actually were working mothers reacted just as strongly. Diana could not handle everything alone. The children's roles were well defined, giving them the freedom to pursue their own interests while helping out with family chores. Therapists should always be cautious about imposing their own values, particularly when dealing with life problems they have not themselves experienced.

Even the family paradigm does not always hold—families differ widely, and so does what is best in a given case. In the Dougherty family the index patient was the father, Terry, 60, who had been hospitalized for serious depression. During treatment with the family, we discovered his alcoholism. Terry shared a room with the oldest of his five sons. One of the mother's complaints was her fear that the father would "harm" Francis while intoxicated; she wanted Terry to move out of "Francis' room." But this arrangement had continued for ten years, with no sign of violence from the father. Besides, it seemed that Francis felt very close to his father, and that this relationship with his son was one of Terry's few cherished relationships. Francis wanted to continue sharing a room with his father, but he didn't feel free to say so. He feared retaliation from his mother, the strong figure in the family, and the family controller. Only after several discussions was Francis able to express support for his father against his mother, enabling a helpful discussion by all the children of how much they wished Terry could be more a part of their lives.

The paradigm's dictates—to strengthen the boundary between father and son as a strategy for increasing the intimacy of the spouses—would have been inappropriate in this case, in which there was little prospect of building marital intimacy. In the Dougherty case, the proper focus was working with Terry on his drinking problem and working with the parents to increase their effectiveness as a parental team, particularly helping Terry get closer to his children, and helping Meghan deal with the children in a less punitive fashion.

One of Anina Giacomelli's problems was her failure to fulfill the role of a woman in a patriarchal Italian-American family. The appropriate therapeutic intervention was to help her fill the role she saw as hers, rather than working to widen her options, as would be the technique of choice with many women in their late thirties.

It is difficult to overestimate the inertia of a family system. Even the most desired changes do not happen overnight. A period of experimentation and stabilization is always necessary. A wife who has complained for years about having to do all the work will find it extremely difficult to give her recovering husband space to act as husband and father. This is partly the resentment and distrust that have built up, but it is also partly the fact that everything in the family is organized around her taking the executive roles. When the phone rings, she will answer it. If she is downstairs, a child will automatically yell, "Ma, the phone's ringing." It will be a while before everyone remembers that Dad can now be trusted to answer the phone and even take a message. In addition, Mother may find it difficult to utilize her free time and energy. She has spent her life taking care of children and house almost single-handed. Now the children are growing up, and they can help with the housework along with Dad. What are all the things she once wished she had time to do? Therapy may have to focus on helping Mother find a job, or develop a forgotten hobby, just as much as working with Dad to help him maintain sobriety.

When role shifts are necessary, they must be stabilized by new rewards and compensations. We saw similar problems in the Harrison and Williams cases. Clara's coping with Fred's drinking had taken her away from the house, where Mary had taken over. Now Clara wanted to change that, taking on more of what she saw as the role of wife and mother. Mary's compensation was new possibilities for her—attending college full-time instead of only in the evenings. Without some such step, it would have been very difficult for Fred and Clara to move toward each other.

In the Williams case, his parents' increasing intimacy quite literally pushed Bob out of his mother's bed. Janet was able to say, "I need you both," but it was obvious that it would be some time before that perception was assimilated.

In families with recovered alcoholics, like the Harrisons and Williams, the therapist may pinpoint interaction patterns that relate to the active drinking days. It is a matter of interest to family theoreticians how easily "hold-over" patterns can be cleaned up. Often the mildest of interventions are sufficient to spark change. Cognitive interpretations usually have little or no effect on behavior rooted in ongoing structural interactions. Simply pointing out what people are doing has little value. People will agree *ad infinitum* that they are doing something that should be changed, and go right on doing it. But hold-over patterns do often yield to mild interventions.

In one couple I worked with, Howard had been sober for three years. Now he was trying earnestly to improve a marital relationship which had deteriorated while he was drinking heavily. Whenever he tried to talk to Karen, however, she reacted with enormous hostility and resentment. Karen was reacting the way she used to when Howard was drinking. Making her look at this behavior while it was happening helped her to understand that her behavior of the past was inappropriate now, when drinking was not part of interaction. This interpretation encouraged both to work toward the improved relationship they both desired.

Chris comes from a family whose father is an alcoholic. So are most of her uncles. She grew up with a strong sense of anxiety; she never knew if they were going to have enough money to satisfy minimal needs. She learned "men don't give you what you have to have in life. They are not competent."

Chris married Thom, a young foreigner from a traditional, strongly patriarchal family. Thom's father had always supported his family at a high standard of living. Chris and Thom are both working. Thom wants to save a large proportion of their salaries, but Chris can't bear this; she wants to get the things she never had, right away. Any initiative Thom takes to build up financial reserves makes Chris feel deprived. A consequence of this behavior: a continuous put-down of Thom which makes him feel incompetent, unable to fulfill his wife's need.

It took one session to put Chris in touch with the fact that she was organizing her husband according to the image of men she was carrying from her own family of origin. When she became aware of what she was doing, her attitudes modified, and so did her behavior. Realizing that in trying to build together, Thom was trying to provide for her, she was able to join her husband, committing herself to their joint view of future goals.

Jennifer and Gary are a family like the Harrisons in the sense that Gary has already been sober for almost 14 years. But during the drinking years, Jennifer became used to disciplining the children alone in a way in which there was no room for Gary. It took a series of therapeutic sessions to give the family an experience of Gary acting as father. As Jennifer made space for him, they reestablished the parental system with the incorporation of a well-functioning adult man. Once the experience was possible, change proceeded rapidly. Excluding Gary was a habit, not a pattern relevant to the present. Family systems have great inertia, but they are also responsive to current input. Working in the present with the present interactions can spark therapeutic change.

For convenience's sake, most of the therapeutic strategies considered in this book have been written around the "normal" American nuclear family. However, the principles involved are general enough to apply to any family form. Two women pooling their income, sharing an apartment with both sets of children, may need the same help learning to work effectively as a parental team that a husband and wife seek. A couple who have both been married before will have to go about the same tasks of building a spouse relationship as the most inexperienced newlyweds.

The therapist working with alcoholic families will see the whole variety of extended, broken and blended families, each facing the problems of their particular "family shape," compounded by the problems of alcoholism. Whatever the family shape, people are still "more human than otherwise." Adults need the support and companionship of other adults. They need their own interests and gratifications. Children need the security of parental discipline to be able to grow and explore. The family is usually the best possible source for meeting these needs.

If problems cannot be met within the family unit, substitutes may have to be found. Individual therapy may have to substitute for parental guidance, as was happening in the Richardson case. Sometimes a multiple family group can be useful in providing surrogate parents and siblings.

The Stephens family entered therapy six months after the father stopped drinking. They stopped after a few sessions, feeling they could organize the family in the way they both wanted.

A few years later, Linda called me, asking for a session with her two daughters. Mark had left her and was living with another woman. They would be married this summer. Linda was having difficulty coping with the girls, now 10 and 12. In this case, therapy focused on helping Mark and Linda develop a relationship in which they could continue to act as the girls' parents. The girls had to begin to accept the father's remarriage and let their stepmother into their lives. An important step was helping Linda conquer her sense of being in competition with Mark's new wife, so as to establish a more secure parental system for the girls.

It seems unnecessary to give many examples of boundary drawing because most of the work described in the case examples focused on this. I want to warn the reader that this important work can seem like the essence of the mundane. Boundary making can easily focus on who's going to take out the garbage—a far cry from the vivid drama of the Oedipal complex and the psychoses and neuroses of individual psychodynamic therapy. But "life is what goes on while you're making plans," and it is work with the mundane events of life that is the stuff of building and repairing families.

In conclusion, a therapist must respect her clients. There are some people who cannot or will not change. All families are hampered in changing—they can at best move only in certain directions. Ideally, the therapist will be flexible enough to help an individual family change in whatever the best direction is for them.

Bibliography and Recommended Reading

Family Therapy

Haley, Jay. *Problem Solving Therapy.* San Francisco: Jossey Bass Publishers, 1976.

Haley, Jay. *Changing Families—A Family Therapy Reader.* New York: Greene & Stratton, 1971.

Laqueur, H. Peter. "General System Theory, and Multiple Family Therapy." In *Current Psychiatric Therapies.* Vol. 8. New York: Greene & Stratton, 1968.

Laqueur, H. Peter. "Mechanisms of Change in Multiple Family Therapy." In *Progress in Group and Family Therapy,* ed. Clifford J. Sager et al. New York: Brunner-Mazel, 1972.

Minuchin, Salvador. *Families and Family Therapy.* Cambridge: Harvard University Press, 1974.

Minuchin, Salvador et al. *Psychosomatic Families.* Cambridge: Harvard University Press, 1978.

Minuchin, Salvador et al. *Family Therapy Techniques.* Cambridge: Harvard University Press, 1981.

Siegel, Leonard and Celia Dulfano. "Family Therapy: An Overview." In *Career Directions,* published by Sandoz Pharmaceuticals, Vol. II, No. 6, 1972.

Siegel, Leonard and Celia Dulfano. "Multimodal Psychotherapy." In *Group Process Today, Evaluation and Perspective*, Donald Milman et al. Springfield: Charles E. Thomas, 1974.

Alcoholism — Books

Cohen, Pauline and Merton S. Krause. *Casework with Wives of Alcoholics*. New York: Family Service Association of America, 1971.

Estes, Nada J. and M. Edith Heinemann. *Alcoholism, Development, Consequences and Interventions*. St. Louis: The C.V. Mosby Co., 1977.

Filstead, Williams et al. *Alcohol and Alcohol Problems: New Thinking and New Directions*. Cambridge: Ballinger Publishing Co., 1976.

Glatt, Max. "A Family Illness." In *The Alcoholic and the Help He Needs*. New York: Taplinger Publishing Co., Inc., 1974.

Goodwin, Donald. *Is Alcoholism Hereditary?* New York: Oxford University Press, Inc., 1976.

Heyman, Margaret. *Alcoholism Programs in Industry*. New Brunswick: Rutgers Center of Alcohol Studies, 1978.

Johnson, Vernon E. *I'll Quit Tomorrow*. New York: Harper and Row, 1973.

Kalant, Harold et al. *Drugs, Society and Personal Choice*. Don Mills: Paper Backs, 1971.

Kaufman, Edward and Pauline N. Kaufman. *Family Therapy of Drug and Alcohol Abuse*. New York: Gardner Press Inc., 1979.

Kissin, Benjamin and Henri Begleiter. *Treatment and Rehabilitation of the Chronic Alcoholic*. New York: Plenum Publishing Co., 1977.

Marblatt, Alan G. and Peter E. Nathan, eds. *Behavioral Approaches to Alcoholism*. New Brunswick: Rutgers Center of Alcohol Studies, 1978.

Pattison, E. Mansell et al. *Emerging Concepts of Alcohol Dependence*. New York: Springer Publishing Co., 1977.

Paolino, Thomas J., Jr. and Barbara S. McCrady. *The Alcoholic Marriage*. New York: Greene & Stratton, 1977.

Zimberg, Sheldon et al. *Practical Approaches to Alcoholism Psychotherapy*. New York: Plenum Publishing Co., 1978.

Alcoholism — Articles and Chapters

Ablon, Joan. "Family Structure and Behavior in Alcoholism: A review of the literature." In *The Biology of Alcoholism*, Vol. 4., Benjamin Kissin and Henri Begleiter. New York: Plenum Publishing Co., 1974.

Ablon, Joan. "Al-Anon Family Group." In *American Journal of Psychotherapy*, 28:1, January, 1974. pp. 30-45.

Bacon, Selden M. "Excessive Drinking and the Institution of the Family." In *Quarterly Journal of Studies on Alcohol Education*, Yale Summer School of Alcohol Studies, New Haven, 1945.

Bateson, Gregory. "The Cybernetics of 'Self': A Theory of Alcoholism." In *Psychiatry*, 34, February, 1971, pp. 1-18.

Berenson, David. "Alcoholism in the Family System." In *Family Therapy: Theory and Practice*, ed. Philip Guerin, Jr., Gardner Press, 1976.

Blum, Eva Marie. "Psychoanalytic Views of Alcoholism." In *Quarterly Journal of Studies on Alcohol*, 27:3, June, 1966.

Bowen, Murray. "Alcoholism as Viewed Through Family Systems Theory and Family Psychotherapy." In *The Person with Alcoholism*, eds. Frank A. Seixas et al. New York: New York Academy of Sciences, 1974.

Bush, Preston Florence. "Combined Individual, Joint and Group Therapy in the Treatment of Alcoholism." In *Differential Diagnosis and Treatment in Social Work*, Francis J. Turner. The Free Press, 1968.

Carter, Elizabeth. "Generation after Generation—The long-term treatment of an Irish family with widespread alcoholism over multiple generations." In *Family Therapy, Full Length Case Studies*, ed. Peggy Papp. New York: Gardner Press Inc., 1977.

Cork, R. Margaret. *The Forgotten Children*. Addiction Research Foundation, Toronto, 1968, 112 pp. (Also in paperback edition.)

Cotton, Nancy S. "The Familial Incidence of Alcoholism— A Review." In *Journal of Studies on Alcohol*, Vol. 40, No. 1, 1979.

Edwin, J.A. and R.E. Fox. "Family Therapy of Alcoholism." In *Current Psychiatric Therapies*, ed. J.H. Masserman. New York: Greene & Stratton, 1968.

Esser, P.H. "Conjoint Family Therapy with Alcoholics." In *British Journal of Addiction*, 1971, pp. 66, 251-255.

Finlay, Donald G. "Effect of Role, Network Pressure on an Alcoholic's Approach to Treatment." In *Social Work*, 11:4, October, 1966.

Fox, Ruth. "The Alcoholic Spouse." In *Neurotic Interaction in Marriage*, copyright by Basic Books, 1956, 21 pp. Reprint.

Gorad, Stephen L. "Communicational Styles and Interaction of Alcoholics and Their Wives." In *Family Process*, 10:4, December, 1971, pp. 475-489.

Jackson, Joan K. "The Adjustment of the Family to the Crisis of Alcoholism." In *Quarterly Journal of Studies on Alcohol*, 15:4, December, 1954, pp. 562-586.

Jantzen, Curtis. "Families in the Treatment of Alcoholism." In *Journal of Studies on Alcohol*, 38:1, January, 1977, pp. 114-130.

Meeks, Donald et al. "Family Therapy with the Families of Recovering Alcoholics." In *Quarterly Journal of Studies on Alcohol*, 31:2, June, 1970, pp. 339-413.

Miller, Peter M. et al. "A Social Learning Approach to Alcoholism Treatment." In *Social Casework*, May, 1974.

Price, Gladys M. "Alcoholism is a Family Illness." In *Casework Papers*, 1960. Reprint copyrighted by the Family Service Association of America.

Social Casework—Special Issue, January, 1978, Vol. 59, No. 1. *Dimensions of Alcoholism Treatment*.

Steinglass, Peter. "Experimenting with Family Treatment Approaches to Alcoholism, 1950-1975: A Review." In *Family Process*, 15:1, March, 1976, pp. 97-123.

Steinglass, Peter et al. "A System Approach to Alcoholism." In *Archives of General Psychiatry*, Vol. 24, May, 1971.

Steinglass, Peter et al. "Interactional Issues as Determinants of Alcoholism." In *American Journal of Psychiatry*, 128:3. September, 1971.

Steinglass, Peter et al. "An Experimental Treatment Program for Alcoholic Couples." In *Journal of Studies on Alcohol*, Vol. 40, No. 3, 1979.

Steinglass, Peter et al. "Alcoholism and the Family, A Review." In *Marriage and Family Review*, Vol. 2, No. 41, 1979.

Steinglass, Peter et al. "A Life History of the Alcoholic Family." In *Family Process*, Vol. 19, No. 3, 1980.

Strayer, Robert. "The Social Worker's Role in Handling the Resistance of the Alcoholic." In *Differential Diagnosis and Treatment in Social Work*, J. Francis Turner. The Free Press, 1968.

Ward, Robert F. et al. "The Alcoholic and His Helpers." In *Quarterly Journal of Studies on Alcohol*, 31:3, September, 1970, pp. 684-691.

Wolin, Steven J. et al. "Families' Rituals and the Recurrence of Alcoholism over Generations." In *American Journal of Psychiatry*, 136, 1979, pp. 589-593.

Wolin, Steven J. et al. "Disruptive Family Rituals—A Factor in the Intergenerational Transmission of Alcoholism." In *Journal of Studies on Alcohol*, Vol. 41, No. 3, 1980.